# The Significance of the Landscape
# Switzerland — Vacationland

# Focus on Switzerland

Arrow pointing the way to the Alpine huts Devil's Bridge from "Itinera Alpina" by J.J. Scheuchzer, 1723                    p. 2

View from the Säntis towards the Stockberg featuring the Lüstispitz and the Risi Pass                    p. 6

4

# TABLE OF CONTENTS

# THE SIGNIFICANCE OF THE LANDSCAPE

Hans Weiss

## The Natural Landscape

What does "landscape" mean? We feel that we know what it signifies. For most of us, the word conjures up some tangible image — the recollection of a particular country scene, the view from one's own window or from that of a moving train. But if one looks for an all-embracing definition, difficulties begin to arise. Is landscape something objective, such as the aspect of a particular section of the earth's surface, or is it primarily the subjective experience which we feel when we become aware of our environment?

And if we are disposed for the moment to leave the question open, further distinctions may come to mind. To many people, landscape means the countryside as distinct from the town. To them, it is therefore only that part of our environment which is not built over, and where natural elements, such as climate, geological forces, erosion, contours and vegetation are the dominant features. Others again consider that the landscape is merely that part of the earth's surface which has been planted and cultivated. I recall a conversation with a farmer in the Val Onsernone, a remote valley in the Ticino, when I was enthusiastically admiring the steep, pine-covered sides of the valley and the waterfalls; for him this was not landscape at all, but merely

"nature" and he could think of nothing more repulsive! Does this imply that the idea of a beautiful landscape is in the last resort no more than a dream of some lost paradise? Does it, from the mountain farmer's point of view, mean simply a garden with its existence perpetually menaced by natural forces? Or, to put it another way, is the landscape not really a garden, but merely the visible evidence of nature with which the people in the towns have lost contact and which has no relevance to their daily lives? In fact, there are many city-dwellers who are no longer in direct contact with nature, for whom the idea of landscape is synonymous with the idea of "nature" — a meadow full of wild flowers, or perhaps the forests, a lake and mountains. It is only when one is out of contact with nature that one begins to appreciate its full significance and the rural aspect of the country. At any rate this is the case for millions of visitors and tourists who come to Switzerland. Many regions in other countries have appropriated the designation "Switzerland" for some unspoilt region of mountains — "Saxon Switzerland". "Chilean Switzerland" and the like. And even the farmer for whom the countryside which delights our eyes means weary toil, danger and catastrophe, and who would never climb a mountain for pleasure, he, too, will display somewhere in his living quarters a faded calendar illustration of a forest in a riot of autumn colouring or a picture postcard showing the glow of the setting sun on the mountains. It is possible that this idealistic picture of the

Hans Weiss, Director of the Swiss Institute for the Preservation and Care of the Landscape, Bern

The Hill Castles of Valeria and Tourbillon                p.8

country helps him to put up with his arduous existence.

For people who live in cities, their idea of the country can hardly be expected to correspond with any objective reality. Large-scale industrial complexes and housing estates for their workers were established in Switzerland at the beginning of the industrial age; following the main traffic arteries of the central plains, they gradually merged into conurbations.

Large parts of Switzerland however, of which the Alps and the Jura are the most important, are still only partially inhabited, even today. Yet the whole country, apart from a few small areas and excluding the glaciers and hard rock, has received the imprint of human hands; unremitting toil down the centuries has wrested from their natural state meadows, fields and pastures. The fingers of the glacier behind Zmutt, near Zermatt, lie at the same level as the former cornfields — hardly larger than a table-cloth — which cling to the sun-baked rocks. And even today in the dark gorges of the infant Rhine in the high Alps, in the Versamer torrent, the farmer descending from his village can mow the grass which will be stored to feed his cattle during the winter.

Long before the industrial era man had therefore started to modify the landscape. Even that of the Swiss National Park, created in 1919, is no pristine natural landscape. Large parts of it have been extensively cultivated for centuries past. Where the forest was cut down to provide charcoal and for iron smelting, no jungle has grown up in its place, but only grassland and the slender mountain pine. And even as recently as 1959 the Swiss electorate, after a hotly-contested campaign, gave only a small majority vote in favour of a hydro-electric development project for the Spöl which flows through the

Houses harmonizing with the landscape. View of Speicher (Appenzell). Panel painting, early 19th century.

National Park; since completion of the Engadine power scheme the Spöl has become a reservoir, below which it turns into a gentle
stream, while its main waters are channelled
through underground pipes to supply electric
power for the factories, and light and heat for
the lowland population.

When the tribes of Central Europe ceased their
nomadic existence and became sedentary, cut
down the forest and began systematically to till
the land and to rear cattle, Switzerland became
an agricultural country, with a cultivated landscape.

The land area is today divided up as follows:

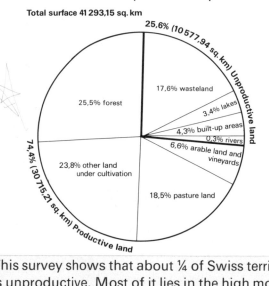

Total surface 41 293,15 sq. km

25,6% (10 577,94 sq. km) Unproductive land

17,6% wasteland

3,4% lakes

4,3% built-up areas

0,3% rivers

6,6% arable land and vineyards

25,5% forest

74,4% (30 715,21 sq. km) Productive land

23,8% other land under cultivation

18,5% pasture land

This survey shows that about ¼ of Swiss territory
is unproductive. Most of it lies in the high mountain areas consisting of rock, boulders and glaciers. Almost ¾ of Switzerland, i.e. all the rest,
with the exception of built-up areas and communications, has for centuries been developed for
agriculture and afforestation.

With the coming of the industrial age, nature
was further reduced to isolated stretches of
what used to be a continuous area of virgin landscape — wild grassland on rocky slopes, rubble

Storm clouds over the Lake of Geneva

brought down by avalanches, swamps on the higher ground and the last undrained marshes of the lowlands. Now only the barren, uninhabited high mountain regions can give us an impression of what the primeval landscape was like, the landscape typical of the whole of Switzerland more than 20,000 years ago.

The southward view from the Jungfraujoch shows nothing but an expanse of rock and ice broken only by the highest peaks emerging from it. It is hardly possible to believe that we are anywhere near to the Rhone Valley far below with its vineyards and apricot orchards; one has the feeling of being transported, at least in spirit, back to the Ice Age. Anyone who thinks that Switzerland consists primarily of mountain peaks, glaciers and waterfalls will feel some disappointment when landing at the intercontinental airport of Geneva-Cointrin or Zurich-Kloten and continuing by bus or train through the Central Lowlands which the French-speaking Swiss so aptly term the "Swiss plateau". Actually these Central Lowlands, in which three-quarters of Switzerland's population live and work, are by no means flat, but mostly undulating. There are many ranges of hills traversed by winding rivers; in other parts, the country is terraced, or its level parts are dotted with innumerable hillocks, formed by the moraines of the Ice Age glaciers. But the higher parts of the Central Lowlands never reach any great height, and there are no glaciers at all. Even so, anyone taking the trouble to climb up to one of these higher points on a clear day will be most amply rewarded. On most of the more prominent ridges of the Central Lowlands one has the impression of being in the centre of a huge bowl, its southern or eastern edges formed by the peaks of the Alpine ranges. To the Dutchman, coming from a country with no mountains at all, the snow-capped peaks sparkling in the summer sun seem like a wonder of nature. To the Norwegian, used to deep fjords and towering rock-faces with a succession of glaciers, the 3,000-metre and 4,000-metre peaks of the Swiss Alps may not seem anything special. Gazing at the Alps from the Central Lowlands, he will scarcely imagine that the Swiss peaks rise above the level where he is standing to twice the height above sea level of the mountains in his own country. Nevertheless, even for the Swiss, the sight of the mountains has something impressive about it, even though he may not be conscious of it in the course of his everyday activities. The Alpine peaks symbolize all that is eternal and immutable in sharp contrast to the constantly changing scene of our surroundings, be it the life of stress in the cities and industrial centres, or the slower, inexorable seasonal variations on the land with their succession of changes in colouring and features. In May the cherry trees, for which the cantons of Zug and Basel-Country are particularly noted, spread their innumerable white blossoms over whole areas of grassland, practically encircling the villages in which one can just make out the church spire and house-tops.

The evergreen spruce is no native of the Central Lowlands; in many regions it has been planted over wide areas and the forests where it predominates have a very monotonous effect. But in those regions where the original deciduous forests still exist, consisting of beech, ash, maple, oak and an occasional wild cherry, we can observe the seasonal changes in colour and shape almost from one day to another, from the bright green of the first foliage of the birch tree to the golden yellow and rich crimson of most deciduous trees in the autumn. And beyond this foreground, there stand the Alps with their eternal snows. They can be seen from those observation points which are the goal of so many outings and at least one of which is close to every large Swiss town. For Zurich it is the Uetliberg, the Gurten at Bern, the Dreiländerblick at St. Gall, the broad ridges at Schaffhausen from which one can see not only the Alps but also the Hegau in Germany, and the Salève at Geneva, its limestone layers standing out clearly from between the trees, showing that we are no longer in the Central Lowlands but at the point where the Jura mountains begin.

Basel, a city which from time immemorial has always been inclined to go its own way geographically, politically and culturally, is the only Swiss city that turns its back on the Alps and faces northwards towards Alsace in France, the Upper Rhine plain and the Black Forest of South Germany. Basel is separated from the Central Lowlands and the rest of Switzerland by the Jura mountains. By way of compensation, Basel has the Rhine, its turbulent waters flowing northwards towards the wide world beyond. This is where Switzerland has built up part of its merchant fleet, hardly comparable, of course, to that of a maritime nation. But in the Rhine Harbour of Basel one has the sensation of being nearer to the sea than to the Alps.

But we seem to have strayed somewhat from the real theme of this chapter, the natural landscape of Switzerland. It is not the green fields, the blossoming fruit trees, the vineyards, the fields of maize and corn of the Central Lowlands, and it is certainly not the towns, conurbations and villages. Where, then, in Switzerland, can we find the real virgin country? It may seem paradoxical that Switzerland, widely regarded as the classical landscape country, should have left only a few small regions of natural landscape in the strict sense, untouched, or scarcely touched, by human hands, apart from the high Alps themselves. We have mentioned the types of such virgin countryside. But it is not surprising that these are to be found only in a few scattered residual areas, for Switzerland is one of the most densely populated countries in the world and its inhabited area is poor in mineral resources. For this reason it became necessary to utilize the land to the last square yard, from the allotments along the railway embankment right up to the Alpine pastures lying at the highest possible level, alongside the moraines, tarns and glaciers. Even in these unproductive areas, the names of the peaks have been derived from the cultivated Alpine regions: the well-known Piz Palü on the border between the Grisons and Italy got its name from a marshy Alpine meadow. And the Alphubel, rising to 4,000 metres in the Valais Alps, has no grass at all, but only snow and ice, though locally, the word "alp" means the summer pastures on the upper slopes. The innumerable turquoise-coloured *Schotte* lakes are usually to be found above the levels of the cultivated Alpine meadows. The *Schotte* is the liquid matter remaining after cheesemaking and from which the tasty whey is produced. The Milchspüeler lake, lying at the foot of the Kärpfstock in the canton of Glarus, is a reminder that this is the region from which comes the best and most famous *Kräuterzieger* (whey mixed with herbs) in the world.

"Primeval" Switzerland

Two circumstances justify us in speaking of the natural landscape of Switzerland, despite the fact that, in comparison with many other countries, the land has been so much cultivated and planted as to give the impression that the whole country is one vast garden of fields, Alpine pasture and forest.

In the first place, there are still fortunately a few

small pieces of virgin country left, even in the valley-bottoms, which have been considered worth protecting from the aggressive demands of technical and industrial progress. As examples we would mention the Pfynwald, a cone-shaped heap of rubble covered by conifers standing in the middle of the Rhone Valley; the Kloten marshes with some rare examples of marsh and pond vegetation lying right in front of the airstrips of the Zurich international airport; and the Bolle di Magadino, a conservation area in the marshy delta where the Ticino river runs into Lake Maggiore, a bird sanctuary providing safe nesting and breeding places for wildfowl in which many rare and protected plants grow unmolested.

Secondly, the high Alps themselves lying above the Alpine meadows can also be reckoned as forming part of the virgin country of Switzerland, at least as far as they have not been developed by aerial cableways and ski-lifts for the benefit of tourism; some of the peaks and areas of everlasting snow are covered with them like a spider's web and at week-ends and during the winter sports season the ski enthusiasts foregather in droves.

Beyond a height of 2,500 metres above sea level the mountains show hardly any signs of human activity, perhaps only a few traces almost insignificant against the towering mass of the mountains – a hut erected by the Swiss Alpine Club, built entirely from local stone and scarcely distinguishable against the background of rock; or a signpost along a mountain trail, often interrupted and occasionally little more than a natural ledge of rock or a mountain stream, a marker sign in the form of a heap of stones loosely piled together, the so-called

Vegetation of pre-glacial Switzerland, from "Urwelt der Schweiz" by Oswald Heer, 1865

The Zermatt glacier (Valais). Detail from a lithograph by Louis Agassiz, 1840

*Steinmännli* (stone man), to help the mountaineer to find his way, even in mist or driving snow. All the high Alps are considered to form the so-called "unproductive areas". Together with lakes, they make up around 25% of the total land surface of Switzerland. The term "unproductive area" may seem to reflect to some extent the proverbial and frequently criticized urge of the Swiss to make money. Anything not showing an immediate profit is regarded as unproductive. But in more recent times, it has been demonstrated how even barren regions of snow-covered mountains can be turned to advantage by attracting the open-handed tourist or being converted into stored electrical power.

We shall have more to say about the Alps in a later section. Here it is sufficient to refer to this remaining 25% of continuous virgin Swiss landscape which has now become the scene of a completely different type of productive activity, one which cannot be measured in economic terms. Far removed from the civilizing activities of the technocrat and the division of labour which characterizes them, men and women can find ample space for recreation, a bountiful opportunity to commune with themselves and to enjoy unspoilt country. Here there is not only a difference of environment, but time takes on another rhythm. There are scarcely any of the subtle seasonal changes, only tiny Alpine flora pushing out their shoots, the glacier crowfoot *(ranunculus glacialis)* dotted over the faces of the Finsteraarhorn up to a height of 4,000 metres, and from the hollows often lying beneath deep masses of snow, the first shrill squeaking of the marmots heralds the end of the long winter. But apart from the elementary life of the high Alps, the mountain landscape generally remains unaltered. There has been virtually no change since the end of the last Ice Age some 20,000 years ago.

Let us pause for a while in the "primeval world of Switzerland"; a book with this title *(Urwelt der Schweiz)* was published in 1865, the same year that Edward Whymper made his famous first ascent of the Matterhorn which ended so tragically, and which saw the start of the golden age of mountaineering. In this work, long since superseded by more learned accounts but which remains unsurpassed for its graphic descriptions, the natural history research scholar from Glarus, Oswald Heer, Professor of Botany at Zurich University, describes the Swiss landscape with its flora and fauna at the close of the geological era of which the Ice Age referred to just now is, so to speak, the last few minutes.

Here are described the tropical marshes of the Carboniferous Age, the coral islands of the lakes of Jurassic rock and chalk. Millions of years ago, prehistoric cattle and elephantine mammals wandered freely over the country of the Zurich uplands. Johann Jakob Scheuchzer came to the conclusion that the fossilized remains discovered near Oensingen in 1727 were the "skeleton of a human being drowned during the Flood". Oswald Heer, however, more correctly from the paleontological aspect, recognized them as those of a giant lizard, all of which in no way lessens the fascination to be obtained from such discoveries.

I still remember clearly the moment when two younger colleagues and I dug out at the foot of an overhanging wall of sandstone a blackish object which seemed unusually hard and heavy. Undoubtedly it was a bone. But it could not be part of an animal which had recently died, since it was fossilized. Also it must have been at least as old as the rock from which we had dislodged it. As we were to discover later, it was a bone

Sorting out auriferous gravel in the Upper Valais in the early 16th century. Woodcut from Sebastian Münster's "Cosmographia universalis", 1544

from the centre of the foot (metatarsus) of a rhinoceros which used to roam in the area some 20 million years ago. At that time what are now the Central Lowlands of Switzerland must have been part of a sub-tropical zone. Even today at the base of the same sandstone rock there are a large number of finely-grained imprints of the leaves from the cinnamon *(cinnamomum)* tree of that age. Many other discoveries of plant and animal remains confirm the reconstructed picture of this region during the Tertiary Period, i.e. prior to the Ice Age and during and after the period when the Alps were folding into shape – a vast expanse of swamp, lagoons, tropical and, later, sub-tropical vegetation, broad rivers and enormous stretches of lake. The sandstone ridge above the place where we made our find is nothing else but the solidified cross-section of a channel carved by a river, the waters of which brought stones, sand and mud from the Alpine ranges, then in process of being formed, down into the lower regions. Cinnamon leaves and rhinoceros bones were the flotsam of this mighty watercourse deposited by chance at the spot where we found them 20 million years later.

Thus we have been making long strides through the historical development of the earth in Switzerland, going back through the mists of time. The variety of the scenery which we have noted all bears out the single characteristic – a prodigious variety within a very limited area. We come across this variety again and again, not only in consecutive stages of time, but also in the vertical cross-sections through the earth. Emil Egli, the geographer and ecologist, writes:

Earliest representation of a climbing-iron, by the naturalist Johann Jakob Scheuchzer, early 18th century

"Switzerland is a small country, but she has extensive areas rising vertically. Features widely spread over the surrounding regions of Europe are pushed up close together in the Alps and concentrated into compact areas. Between the lowest ground and the peaks exceeding 4,000 metres above sea level lies an almost baffling agglomeration of geological strata".

To take one illustration, the view southwards from the Jungfraujoch embraces not only the Ice Age of long ago but also the arctic landscape of Greenland. So far as they have not been artificially irrigated by the melting waters from the glaciers, the slopes overlooking the Rhone Valley are dry steppe areas of grass and bush which otherwise flourish only in a dry Mediterranean climate.

## Land of Natural Contrasts

Extremes of temperature and rainfall are to be found in close proximity to each other. A distance of only 40 kilometres as the crow flies separates the grassland of the rocky areas in the dry climate of Stalden (Valais) from the Monte Moro Pass, where the ridge of the Alps acts as a rain trap. Here the falls of rain and snow are of monsoon proportions and the annual rainfall amounts to 4 metres or more, whereas in the former area it is no more than 52 centimetres. The latter is the same as the rainfall of the Hungarian *puszta* and of even larger areas of steppe country. And in the Bergell region of the Grisons, the dazzling granite peaks, with their glaciers creeping down wild gorges, soar straight up from the midst of the chestnut forests of Castasegna and the vineyards of the Chiavenna Valley.

The palm trees and gardens on the Brissago Islands (Lake Maggiore) may remind some people of Spain or Italy; those not familiar with these countries could regard them as places of eternal spring and tropical profusion. And what a contrast to the landscape of the passes which, though not strictly belonging to the high Alps, nevertheless mostly lie above the tree limit, leaving only small patches for vegetation. To quote the botanist Walter Rytz: "The region of the Gotthard Hospice seems at first sight to be quite barren of vegetation. Here there are hardly any of the real Alpine meadows such as those elsewhere that delight the eye with their colouring. On the contrary, one might imagine oneself to be transported to the far north, Lapland perhaps. Furthermore, the features of the landscape fit this image perfectly, the gentle hillocks, the bare humps, relics from the Ice Age and the soft mountain contours. And finally, the types of flora to be found here are unmistakable to the expert eye; what he beholds is a field of northern flora."

Farm-house in Valmaggia (Ticino)

*Montanvert  
Juillet 1891*

*Col de Balme. Juillet. 1891*

Album leaf with dried Alpine flowers

The Martagon lily, one of the finest protected specimens of Alpine flora.
English lithograph, 1820

It is not only North and South which meet in Switzerland, but also East and West. There is a marked difference between the continental climate of the high valley of the Engadine, where the hot summer and autumn give place to the very cold, clear skies of the winter, beneath the vault of that azure blue colouring which gives its name to the valley, and the climate of the northern slopes of the Alps where the dampness from the oceans is completely different from the neighbouring valleys of the inner Alps.

## The Föhn

Another feature peculiar to Switzerland which merits a more detailed description is the *föhn*. Through the Alpine valleys running north to south, it brings to the Central Lowlands a warm wind with an effect similar to that of the Gulf Stream on the west coasts of Britain and Scandinavia, even though climatically it is a quite different phenomenon. The *föhn* sweeps down as a southerly wind over the Alpine range. The air current is generated when low temperatures in the north coincide with a high temperature in the south. On the south of the Alps, the air becomes cooler as it rises and releases humidity. This causes the monsoon-type rainfalls on the southern slopes. When it blows down the northern slopes, the temperature of the wind rises substantially, sucking up all moisture, so that the *föhn* used to be described loosely as "Sahara air". The temperature can rise by as much as one degree for every hundred metres fall in height, so that local temperatures in the narrow Alpine valleys and foothills can reach summer levels as early as March or as late as November. The improved climatic effect is very obvious; chestnut trees are to be found in the Domleschg, the name for the Rhine Valley (Hin-

terrhein) in the Grisons, and along the fjord-like Walensee, and in midsummer there appear in the forests of that area the red and white cyclamen blossom which usually occurs only in sub-Mediterranean countries.

Hardly any other natural phenomenon has the same effect as the *föhn*. In the spring, which should herald the coming of summer to the mountains, the sun's rays acting on the mantle of snow have little effect until the *föhn* comes. It first casts a thin veil of cloud over the deep blue sky and then blows suddenly with wild, moaning gusts, hot as from an oven, down through the forest into the valley below. What the sun has been unable to achieve is now accomplished in a couple of days. The snow melts under one's gaze, on the mountain slopes it sparkles in the crystal-clear air and during the afternoon a sullen roar like thunder, sometimes near, sometimes far, accompanies the avalanches cascading through well-worn channels down to the valley below, bringing enormous quantities of snow and rubble in their wake. The white mantle of snow is broken up into a few isolated patches, and no sooner has the snow melted away than the Alpine meadows immediately appear with a thin carpet of delicate flowers and rich grass.

In his novel *Peter Camenzind,* Hermann Hesse has given an inimitable description of the *föhn.* "The blue-green waters of the lake are transformed in a few moments into an inky blackness on which suddenly eddies of white foam are lashed up. Soon the lake, which a few minutes before looked so calm and peaceful, casts its waters on the shore with a thunderous roar like ocean waves beating on the coast. At the same time the whole countryside becomes

Specimens of Swiss fauna, by the naturalist Conrad Gessner, 16th century

alarmingly clear. On the peaks which otherwise brood in the distance, it is almost possible to make out details of the rock formation, and villages which looked like a brown patch in the distance, now reveal every roof, gable and window. Everything, mountains, fields and buildings, seems to come closer together, like an alarmed herd of cattle. And then comes a sullen

moaning and the very ground seems to tremble. The waters from the lake are whipped up over a wide area forming what looks like wisps of smoke rushing through the air and all the time, particularly during the night, one can hear the noise of the unceasing battle between the storm and the mountains."

## What is a Landscape?

We have now given a survey of the physical features of the Swiss landscape and some typical examples, from its geological origins and its development down the ages. But we have left unanswered the original question "What is a landscape?"

Gentiana insignis alpina floribus aureis.

Instead of picturesque descriptions, we could have quoted figures and tables which would have given a much more accurate description of the geological formation, the chemical and physical characteristics of the soil, the water supply, the different undulations from the softly-shaped moraines in the Central Lowlands, the chalky landscape of the Jura, the jagged outlines of the pointed rock and the chalk cliffs of the Alpine foothills up to the crystalline pyramids of the Gotthard and Aare massifs. We could have given a systematic account of the plant families and the places where they are to be found. We could, in short, have described all the physical features of our environment which can be measured and mapped. But even so, would this information adequately comprise all that is meant by the Swiss landscape as such? Hardly, since we would have described only the bare essentials. The more statistical detail that is assembled to illustrate the whole picture, the greater the danger that the description of the living landscape will become lost, reduced to a mere abstraction consisting solely of a mass of figures and tabulated data. The computer may well analyse a landscape, but cannot describe it. A description always contains a subjective element and the landscape cannot be considered apart from the people living in it. Its special features take on their individuality only through the experience of human beings, an experience which cannot be computerized, and its individual characteristics appear only through the human influences brought to bear upon them, influences inseparable from Man's origins, his present economic circumstances and his contemporary psyche.

The large gentian. From the cabinet of rarities of a German prince, 18th century

Man's handiwork:
Tilling of the soil on the Swiss Plateau p. 28

# Man in the Landscape

In describing now a few aspects of the "cultivated" landscape of Switzerland, we are thinking not so much of architecture, painting or literature as of the actual cultivation of the land or, in the general, abstract sense of the modern planner, land utilization. For the products resulting from an individual creative process have far less influence on the landscape than natural forces, human tradition and communal activity since these last, though less dramatic, are constantly at work and therefore have more lasting effects.

## Nature as the Deciding Factor

Let us take a simple but very obvious example from the material used in making the roofs of farmhouses. The flagstone roofs of the villages in the mountain valleys of the Ticino are quite steep, but not because of some architectural principle or the individual taste of the local inhabitants, or because here (though some anthropologists have thought so) some prehistoric Ostrogothic influence is being expressed. And the small fields are not enclosed with so many walls because the Ticino population has a "mania for stones". The reasons are much more down to earth. The material which nature has provided in the immediate neighbourhood consists of strata of gneiss rock which can be broken up only into thick slabs, which consequently are very heavy. The roof timbers must therefore be steep and short in order to support the heavy weight of the roofing slabs laid like steps. Here we have an example of how nature has determined the features of houses and human settlements. The villages clinging to the steep mountainsides, their buildings closely grouped round the church, present the appearance of a "roof-scape" to anyone looking down on them from above. The type of roofing stones is in a way merely a more refined reflection of the surrounding rocks.

And how completely different is the appearance of the roofs of houses and farms on the northern Alpine slopes, where the spruce is the predominating type of tree. For years, it has provided the building timbers and the easily shaped logs from which the shingle roofs are prepared, thin wooden boards 30 to 100 centimetres long, with which the structure is roofed over, until they were replaced in many districts by modern materials such as cheap metal plates, earthenware tiles or patent substitutes. In those places where shingle roofs are still in vogue the wood, whitish in its original state, begins to take on a silver-grey tint after the second winter, presenting a very attractive contrast to the black and rust-brown colouring of the sun-scorched wooden walls and to the gentle green of the fields. The region where the spruce shingles originally came from is very extensive and corresponds with the areas where this variety of pine grows most profusely, namely in the high-rainfall valleys of the north-

ern Alps and the high ground over 1100 metres above sea level. In contrast, in the inner Alpine areas where at an altitude of over 1500 metres the larch begins to predominate, its much harder, reddish wood serves as building material. These simple examples of roofing materials show how in Switzerland the outward visible signs of the national styles are often not the expression of some custom or habit, however much we might vaguely feel that it has something to do with "tradition". In fact, the reasons why, for instance, houses are built in a certain style and no other, fields cultivated in a particular way and in no other, are more readily found to be in direct functional relationship to the natural features of the region — relief, soil conditions, climate and vegetation.

Even more effective than rural building traditions is the type and manner of land utilization in shaping the landscape. This time let us take an example from the Central Lowlands. The usual arrangement of fields and meadows in various parts of the Central Lowlands of Switzerland, where strips of land extend radially from some centre, has not been inspired by any peculiar hierarchical tradition; it follows from the three-field rotation system — winter plot, summer plot, fallow. The long, narrow shape of the plots in many parts, referred to half humorously, half in disparagement, as "braces", is the result of re-division of the estate between the heirs for many generations past. In the middle of this "star", nestling among the meadows and fields, lies the village with its church, the whole surrounded by forest and the common land. The common is communally owned for use as pasture and hayfields for all the inhabi-

Ploughed fields by a village on the Swiss Plateau

30

tants. But formerly, even privately owned plots of land were not allowed to be used indiscriminately, as is the case in our own day with its exaggerated deference to the rights of property. In the past, there was a so-called *Flurzwang,* or land control, which obliged the individual farmer to conform with the rotation system and type of cultivation as decided by the community on practical and legal grounds.

This type of landscape with its three-field rotation system still prevails in many districts of the Central Lowlands. It even characterizes the landscape in those places where modern land clearance has been carried out. The radial arrangement of the plots is replaced by a more symmetrical layout with larger fields, like a chessboard. But in the country areas the order from the centre outwards is still: village, field or meadow, pasture or forest.


## The Forest, the Great Constant

We must now say something about the forests. Scattered over the whole country, they cover almost exactly a quarter of the national territory. The forest, too, which as jungle used to cover the whole country with the exception of the lakes, rivers, swamps, rocks and glaciers, has long since been subject to the orderly cultivation of a landscaped countryside. Forestry certainly belongs to the type of land use which in Switzerland is the closest to nature, but the forests are more like tastefully laid-out parkland compared to the remains of what used to be a continuous wilderness of dense jungle. When, during the 19th century, the uncontrolled felling of timber in the mountain forests caused wild torrents to pour forth, flooding the Alpine foothills and bringing widespread death and destruction in their train, the Federal Parliament passed a forestry law which was a piece of pioneer legislation in a country where local politics play a large part. Its effect on land planning is still evident in our own day, and as a means of protecting and controlling the use of forest resources, it is one of the most effective forestry laws in Europe; it originally dates from the year 1902 though it has since been amended to make its provisions even stricter.

This law brought into force what was then an unusual regulation, namely that all forests were declared to be subject to the control and supervision of the Federal Government. The country was divided into forestry regions and districts administered by the cantonal and local councils, but still subjected to overall control from the central government. Nowadays this type of control has been applied to other matters where it is necessary to enforce regulations imposed for the benefit of the whole country against other interests, where federal control alone can ensure that such regulations are uniformly applied. Throughout the country, forests may be cut down only where an overriding public interest requires it, but at the same time an area similar in size must be designated for new afforestation.

In this way forests which at one time were threatened with destruction have been re-established and extended, so that they now present a well-preserved and healthy element in a countryside subjected to ever-increasing demands for building land. The forest is thus both in time and space the great constant factor of the Swiss landscape, extending from the northwest to the south and east, over an extensive region made up by the three areas of Jura, Central Lowlands and Alps.

The woodcutter. Pin-pricked paper, Singine (Fribourg), early 19th century

Characteristic remote farm in the Jura under the first snowfall

## The Jura Country

We have referred to the type of landscape represented by the three-field rotation system in the Central Lowlands. In the Jura, the fold-mountains bordering Switzerland on its western and northern frontiers, we come to a quite different landscape. The flat Jura heights are fully exposed to the winds and very rugged, despite their lower altitudes as compared with the Alps. In the upper valley of La Brévine, lying a mere 1000 metres above sea level, is the "Swiss Siberia" with danger of frost at all seasons, where temperatures occasionally drop to a record low of minus 40°C. In addition to this unfavourable climate, the sub-soil is little more than a thin layer of porous earth through which the chalky rock pokes out like bones exposed through the holes of cast-off clothing. Characteristic features of the Jura country are the meadows and forest clearings. Just as in the high Alps, here, too, there are meadows where the cattle can graze in the summer, like the plateau of the Franches Montagnes, for instance, extending over 200 square kilometres and used primarily for horse-breeding. The closely-knit village is seldom to be found in the higher Jura regions; instead there are isolated farms, and houses built in rows. The farmer's house usually stands in the shelter of a hollow, half-timbered and built of limestone with a slightly inclined roof. It is a type of structure very much reflecting environmental influences, similar to what we have observed in the high Alps.

## Switzerland is not a Toy-Land

Mountains are thus an inseparable part of the Swiss landscape. Even so the visitor cannot expect to find snow-capped peaks everywhere in Switzerland. And the tourist may also feel some disappointment if he allows himself only two or three days for Switzerland out of a hurried tour through Europe, and still expects to obtain a comprehensive picture of the country. The large variety of souvenirs based on landscape features or the Matterhorn in Walt Disney's Wonderland have little relationship to the reality of the Swiss landscape as a whole; these are but a random and therefore untypical assembly of curiosities which, one and all, answer to mere stereotypes.

Switzerland certainly ranks as a small country, embracing within a confined area a vast number of scarcely conceivable variations. But this variety is neither a result of chance nor a showpiece classified with the precision of a museum catalogue. The reality is that this varied scene has been produced from a dynamic way of life, blended with the local types of landscape, giving the whole its unmistakable individuality. The shepherd blowing his alphorn, the chamois poised on a crag, the evening twilight on the glacier or the edelweiss stuck in the hatband – none of these are typical; the reality is rather more the custom and tradition reflected in the particular features of each area of the country resulting from the interplay of natural and civilizing influences, such as the clustered village and fields of the Central Lowlands, the scattered villages in the pre-Alps or the hamlet grouped round a farming community in the Central Bernese country and the Emmental valley. The typical features are not to be found arranged

like pieces of mosaic over the whole country, but in every case related to a whole region. This is why the cultivated landscape gives the impression of being very extensive, where 20th-century industrial and housing developments have so far left it comparatively undisturbed. But this spaciousness can only be experienced by the unhurried traveller.

A Trip through the Emmental

A good example can be taken from the Emmental. If it is impossible to allow oneself the "luxury" of a walking tour taking several days, then one should at least take the train from Bern to Luzern, not by the main line via Olten, but by the less frequented route via Langnau. If one has a little more time, better still to take the train from Bern to Burgdorf and from there to Langnau and Luzern, so that one can obtain at least a fleeting impression of the lower Emmental Valley. Very soon after leaving the built-up areas of Bern, with motorway connections and tower blocks dominating the scene, we are back in the country of that famous story-teller, Jeremias Gotthelf, a country which has scarcely changed its outward appearance since his days. In contrast to other parts where it is the custom to divide up estates, which meant that the farmer's estate was split up among several heirs, here from the earliest times the estate passed to a single heir, usually the youngest son. This means that the farmstead and its lands have remained a single unit for centuries and still form a characteristic feature of the landscape. In this way there has been a unique continuity, clearly reflected to an impressive degree in the

Trademarks on sacks of corn from the Emmental (Bern), 18th century

Bernese peasant, by Johann Friedrich Hassler, 1840

farmhouses of the Emmental valley. The enormous double-thatched roof reaches almost to the ground at the sides and also extends well down over the gable ends as well. Living quarters, stables and barn are under one roof. Like chicks gathered round the hen, the outbuildings cluster round the main farm building, built in the same style with the same materials and the same type of roof – the granary often richly decorated, the *Stöckli* giving separate living accommodation for the grandparents, and often a workshop, a distillery or a house for the milkmaid and farmhands. Villages in the real sense are absent; each farmstead consists of an individual estate in the countryside with large areas of meadow, fields, pasture and forest grouped round it. The road system has been adapted to this arrangement. Each farm has its own approach road. At first sight the roads seem to have been laid somewhat erratically but on closer examination one can see how they have been carefully built to conform to the lie of the land. Soon our journey leads us to the mountain mass of the Napf; geologically it belongs unmistakably to the Central Lowlands, but with its highest point 1411 metres above sea level, it is nevertheless more characteristic of the pre-Alps. Seen on a relief map of the area, it looks like a crumpled ball of paper. Forests cover almost half the total area, but they are scattered like some delicate piece of lacework. Equally scattered is the maze of innumerable watercourses. These, however, reveal the underlying system which prevails even in this "crumpled paper ball". From the summit of the Napf they flow in all directions as torrents pouring through shady glens towards the larger rivers, the Wigger and Langeten to the north, the Emme to the west and the Little Emme to the east, divided by the watershed between the rivers Aare and Reuss. A country so divided by many valleys, if not by sinuous gorges between mountains and hills is, even in our own times, a formidable hindrance to transport. The agricultural country of the Emmental has preserved its far-reaching economic independence for many centuries and, so far as the farms are concerned, preserved it right up to the present, even though in the larger settlements there has been some industrial activity, such as the watch and clock factories of Sumiswald. The extent to which topography can influence human activity is also illustrated by the fact that the Napf forms part of the important dividing lines between different forms of culture within Switzerland, the line of Brünig-Napf-Reuss. Its dividing influence is in fact greater than that of many a range of the high Alps or even the language frontier between the German and French-speaking populations lying far to the west. Although therefore the Napf is not a boundary between language groups, it does form a more significant division in everyday affairs, separating one set of customs and traditions from the others.

Lake of Luzern

Our journey has taken us across the watershed, and the railway now passes through Entlebuch, in the canton of Luzern. We leave the ranges of the Napf territory and approach the expanse of the Lake of Luzern where the Reuss flows out of it. Despite the broader aspect of the landscape, we are entering, geologically speaking, the Alpine region. It is one of the peculiarities of the Napf that it was never covered by glaciers during the Ice Age. It is nothing more than a huge pile of rubble carried down by the watercourse from the infant Aare, here depositing its flotsam piled up from the Ice Age glaciers of the Aare and Reuss.

Alpine wild flowers. Paper silhouette from the Pays d'Enhaut (Vaud), 19th century

Luzern at the north-west tip of the Lake of the Four Forest Cantons (to give it its local name) has all the atmosphere of a seaboard country, although it is surrounded by the limestone Alps dominated by the Pilatus. In less than two hours' journey by rail we have passed from the Bern region into Central Switzerland by a "back door" route from where we shall be continuing in the next section towards the Gotthard.

But let us pause for a while in this territory of Central Switzerland. Compared with the Emmental, it is rather more difficult to describe in a few sentences; its characteristics are mixed and overlap each other in many places. The variety of country is here not only two-dimensional over the whole region; geographically speaking, it is multi-dimensional. On the mountains overlooking the lake is a succession of geological Alpine strata, a vegetation with partly semi-Mediterranean features, manifesting various national and international influences, for several districts have been engaged in the transit traffic over the Gotthard; Schwyz, Küssnacht-am-Rigi and Altdorf are not simply large villages, but have all the features of small towns with their large patrician houses. And it is as if their international character has imposed itself on the natural countryside. Here, as on the shores of the Walensee, chestnut trees blossom and on the rocky sides of Lake Uri the Scots fir and coarse grass are to be found, while the scenery, with the glaciers of the Urirotstock rising up opposite Tell's Chapel, has all the immensity of a Norwegian fjord.

A Peep into the Engadine

No description of the types of landscape making up Switzerland could fail to include a mention of the famous Engadine architecture expressed in the form of an individualistic traditional housing style of its own. This becomes all the more astonishing when historical research tells us that the so-called "Engadine house" is not particularly old-world but that, compared to the really ancient structures of round-shaped logs or the medieval Gotthard architecture, it is of comparatively recent origin. And when one tries to explain to a non-Swiss "expert" on Switzerland that the Engadine houses are not only not old but were originally not even stone buildings, his surprise usually changes into incredulity. But it is a fact that the design of the Engadine house came into fashion only after the destruction following the Thirty Years' War (1618–1648). Instead of the former stone block construction of the Gotthard style, there came into being houses with an outer wall of stone. The framework of the house was of wood, the walls merely a facade. The use of a stone covering served not only the practical aim of protection against fire, water and cold, but it was influenced by emigrants returning to Switzerland and who, when designing their stone houses, copied the *palazzi* of the aristocracy. And in fact many of the houses in the Engadine present a handsome and dignified exterior enhanced by the ornamentation of the outer wall with graffiti according to the whim of the owner; and if, despite this, the "mansions" of the district present a somewhat harsh and plain aspect, it should be remembered that the floor of the Upper Engadine lies about 1800 metres above sea level. The small windows are built deep inside the walls. In the past they were small holes in the wooden "core" of the house, like loopholes through the outer stone. In contrast to the Jura, the type of settlement is here a closely-built village with only slightly overhanging roofs, looking from a distance like some irregular cubist medley of triangles and squares. The combination of Italianate architecture and Alpine materials is particularly well expressed in the private Engadine houses. No doubt this was the reason behind the description of the Engadine landscape by Friedrich Nietzsche as the mingling of southern warmth and cheerfulness with northern grandeur and severity.

And it is especially in the late autumn, when tourists and other visitors have departed from the valley, and the crystal-clear sky sets up so sharp a contrast between the black shadows of towering mountains and the gleaming of the bare pastures, it is then that the Engadine takes on the appearance of some high plateau of Tibet, with the larches blazing like torches in the evening sun.

Window with graffiti at Rhäzüns (Grisons)

## Farewell to the Cultivated Landscape?

"The type of economic activity determines the aspect of the landscape", affirms Heinrich Gutersohn, the well-known geographer. This is by no means an exaggeration of economic as opposed to cultural influences, but the recognition that our countryside is the result of effective farming economics carried on for centuries past. We have all benefited from this inheritance down to our own day, especially when, as inhabitants of the cities, we visit the country for recreation, or when tourist promotion seeks to attract visitors from both inside and outside Switzerland by the promise of "beautiful scenery".

What is it that we find so harmonious in the cultivated countryside which we fail to find in industrial, urban or purely tourist regions? Is it merely a sensation, a sentimental nostalgia for the past? We find this in many quarters, and then one is inclined to say that, in facing the realities of modern industrial and post-industrial society, we must inevitably abandon a conception of the countryside which belongs to an age that is past. Our present-day way of life and business activity requires a quite different pattern – fields resembling some giant chessboard where modern single-crop farming prevails, the industrial scene with its tall girder masts and high-tension cables bestriding mountains and valleys, broad strips marking a focal point of the motorway system or the scattered out-of-town shopping centres, their car parks glittering with the many-coloured patches of chromium plate. This scene may still hold some fascination for us today. It is both tempting and superficial to declare that we have reached the point of no return and that the landscape of the future will be even more abstract and just as capable of meeting the changes in popular demand and taste.

But anyone going into the matter more deeply finds himself more and more disturbed by the impression that all these strange, new features are not some new order but the signs of an increasing chaos which threatens to overwhelm us. The point I would make is that we have sufficient grounds for doubting the assurance of our prophets and futurists. It is nothing like as simple as they would have us believe. The old cultivated landscape still exercises the same fascination for us. It is impossible for us to dissociate it from a feeling of longing for its unique harmony, a harmony expressive of a significant and permanent equilibrium between nature and people. A harmony which, though undoubtedly complex, has over the centuries constituted a well-developed interrelationship between human activity and natural resources. Whether the technical landscape of tomorrow will still be able to give us wholesome food, adequate housing, meaningful employment and recreation is becoming every day more doubtful, in view of the threatening ecological crisis. Possibly we shall in the not too distant future recognize that we have been too hasty in discarding traditional economic systems and that the cultivated landscape of the past was, at any rate in part, the best of all worlds. Who would feel any confidence in denying this? Who knows whether post-industrial society may not come to the conclusion that our much-vaunted realism is a false ideology? Possibly our reaction is in fact symptomatic of a period on which some future observer will look back as one where a "Stone Age" biology and philosophy prevailed and the human race held the exaggerated opinion that nature existed solely for the satisfaction of

Remote farm in the Upper Ticino

The industrial landscape: oil refinery and motorway with clover leaf
pp. 48-49

human needs; Rachel Carson enlarged on this theme as early as 1962 in *Silent Spring*, a book with revolutionary warnings which, significantly, have found an echo throughout the world.

This prospect makes it all the more worthwhile to take a closer look at the types of cultivated landscape which, in Switzerland as elsewhere, is threatened with rapid decline. What may seem in the context of our ever-changing, fast-developing technology to be pointless and out of date is, when looked at more closely, often the result of an age-old wisdom and tradition, which made the best possible use of the equilibrium between nature and man. The wooden huts of a *Maiensäss* (mountain community) nestling close together in the damp climate of the northern Alps are built of logs, where pine forests prevail, or from larchwood and stone, or wholly from stone in those parts of the Alps where the pine is rare or non-existent. Often the houses of the mountain communities stand in a closely-built row, a very economical arrangement in that they make a clear dividing line, on the one side facing the meadows which are collectively owned, and on the other the private individual fields, making it unnecessary to have more than a few lengths of fencing to prevent cattle straying from the pastures over to the meadows which have still to be mown for hay.

The German-Swiss term *Maiensäss* is the general expression for the cultivated ground lying half-way between the valley floor and the meadows of the high Alps where the farmer can feed his cattle in the early summer and late autumn. These *Maiensässe* settlements are distinguished by a basic uniformity, still differing from valley to valley, of scattered or grouped cottages and stables, as well as by the way in which meadows, fields and forests are distributed. Often the *Maiensässe* lie at a level lower than that of the settlements inhabited all the year round, especially where, because of the local topography, these lie on a higher ledge or

Vine-stock. Silk embroidery, 18th century

The neat pattern of the Lavaux vineyards (Vaud)

50

a terraced slope, not on the valley floor. In the high valleys, as at Juf, in the Avers, where the highest populated farming village in Europe to be inhabited all the year round is situated more than 2000 metres above sea level, the *Maiensässe* are on the same level as the Alpine pastures.

With the modern pattern and mechanization of agriculture, the use of the *Maiensässe* pastures is declining, however, as farmers rely increasingly on tractor and trailer to transport their hay to more modern storage facilities at the outskirts of their villages or down in the valley.

In the same way and for the same economic reasons that determined the ancient *Maiensässe,* there arose the vineyard villages in the Lavaux region, that wide expanse of country sloping down to the Lake of Geneva with the largest area of vineyards in Switzerland, where the houses are grouped in closely-built communities in order to retain as much of the precious soil as possible for intensive vineyard cultivation. In addition there appears a style of architecture displaying many aristocratic features, due to the vineyard owner of old having more ready money available than did the farmer ploughing his fields. This applies not only in the Lavaux, but also in other vineyard areas of Switzerland such as those of Lakes Neuchâtel, Biel and Zurich with their stately half-timbered houses, or in parts of the Grisons. All the villages in the wine-growing region therefore show an urban individuality. The large houses built closely together form what looks more like a town centre than a country village. The symmetrically parcelled-out vineyard hills, their innumerable, robust supporting walls ranged along the slopes, give the vineyard country its unique, unmistakable aspect. This patchwork of small plots covering such a vast expanse of farming land is a monoculture, not that of modern, in-dustrialized agriculture, but an ancient system of cultivation which, for intensity of labour and effort within a confined area, is nowhere surpassed except, perhaps, by the "world wonder" of the Oriental rice-terraces.

## Landscape and National Character

Just as mankind has cultivated the country and transformed it from its original state, so in the reverse direction nature has had its unrelenting effect on mankind. Even though this reverse influence is less easy to discern and generalizations about "national character" are always debatable, there is nevertheless something which defines a human type and distinguishes it from the "neighbour". The Bernese are regarded as being slow. And even though this "slowness" in the local character arises rather from a sober approach to life than from an absence of quick thinking, it nevertheless differs from the unfailing presence of mind of the Appenzell folk who were never mainly cultivators of farmland or solely dairy farmers, but stock-breeders and thus, at the same time, cattle dealers.

In the course of our short and very cursory survey of the varied scene in Switzerland, we have endeavoured to show how man, *as a gregarious being,* has left his mark on the landscape. The role which man, *as an individual,* has played in the landscape, can best be illustrated by journeying through the country itself. For many this finds its most vivid expression in the Alps, since here mankind has had least influence on nature. And – who knows? – perhaps it is here that we meet not only nature at its most primitive, but also our own inner personality.

Architecture blending into the landscape: house-tops in Eastern Switzerland

52

# The Alpine Experience

The Alps take up more than 60% of Swiss territory. This is reason enough for devoting a section to them here.

The Alps have long since ceased to count to any pronounced degree in the intellectual life of Europe. In the social and economic sense they have even become a crisis area so far as neither industry nor tourist traffic has been established there. Switzerland has not been immune to the world-wide flight from the rural areas, as is evident from the dwindling populations, especially in the regions of the Alps and pre-Alps. This emigration has also had repercussions on the landscape; decaying pastures can be found in many of the valleys, wild bushes and young pines growing on the once carefully tended pastures. Many villages are half empty, their houses slowly but surely facing collapse. Since last century, the population of more than half the 3029 communes which make up Switzerland has been falling, although the population of the whole country has trebled. Almost half the population lives in the conurbations of Geneva-Lausanne, the Basel region, Bern, Olten-Aarau and Zurich-Baden, where already the cities are merging into continuous built-up areas. Recent developments, tinged with mounting economic uncertainty have however slowed the exodus to the cities a little, and in a number of instances young people have returned to their villages so as to derive at least partial employment from their houses and land. It would nevertheless be premature to say that the trend towards migration to urban areas has been reversed. The overall movement towards greater economic and social concentration continues. These words written in 1948 by André Siegfried, a Frenchman, in his book "La Suisse – démocratie témoin" remain true today: "Economically it is the plain which is vital, psychologically it is the mountain."

How is one to account for this psychological pre-eminence of the Alps? Most obvious is the fact that the Alps are the backbone of Switzerland, whether from a purely topographical or from an orographical point of view. The high mountains are unproductive; at these rarified heights no extensive vegetation belt can exist. The upper level of the tree-limit varies; so far as it has not been disturbed by previous clearances, it lies at around 1800 metres above sea level in the areas bordering on the Alps, and at 2300 and 2400 metres in the interior of the Alps. The vegetation limit, above which no large area of plant life can grow, coincides almost with the snow-line. That is the height above sea level beyond which snow on the level ground never melts during the summer. This line lies at 2500 metres at the Säntis, where on the Blaugletscher (Blue Glacier) a small field of spruce is able to maintain itself. At the Gotthard the snow-line lies at around 2800 metres and on the Monte Rosa massif, which includes the highest peak in Switzerland, the Dufourspitze (4634 metres), it lies at 3300 metres.

The high mountains are therefore, from the purely physical viewpoint, a desert. Perhaps every nation needs its desert, jungle or lake area as a reminder to the people of their dependence on factors other than those of economics, even in our technical age.

Oak-trees, a typical feature of the Genevese countryside

Gazing at the mountains. Pen drawing by Rodolphe Toepffer, early 19th century

A comfortable flight over the Alps is enough to bring this dependence to the fore. The level of cultivated land devoted to food production is very limited. Even above the highest Alpine pastures, the ice-cover begins and small variations in the average annual temperature or in height are enough to make human survival problematical. In his diary for 1947, the writer Max Frisch describes his impressions of such a flight over the Alpine peaks in the autumn, where the winter snows had already fallen on the slopes away from the sun, and summarizes the recognition of this dependence on physical features in a single phrase: "Our homeland rests on a knife edge." And in fact a reduction in the average annual temperature by a mere two or three degrees would mean that the Alpine glaciers would once again descend to the Central Lowlands and that Zurich, for instance, would not lie at the end of a lake but at the foot of an Arctic glacier. Equally vividly, the Alps bring home our

physical dependence by the regularity with which roads are blocked by landslides or avalanches, or overrun by the sudden flooding of the Alpine torrents which still, even in the Central Lowlands, can have serious repercussions, despite extensive protective works and large-scale afforestation.

But the Alps are not merely a hindrance to transport and a threatening interference with the daily life of the people. They also form a link between peoples and their way of life and encourage commercial exchange, especially through the wide lateral valleys and over the passes. The description of the Alps as the backbone of Switzerland can be enlarged upon still further, as we shall see.

In the centre of the lateral chain the Gotthard massif stands like the hub of a wheel. Within it lies the Urseren Valley, like a chamber from which four doors open on the outside world. To the south is the Gotthard Pass, to the east the Oberalp Pass, to the west the Furka Pass and to the north the Schöllenen gorge. This is the point where the four large Alpine cantons meet, Uri in the centre, Ticino in the south, the Grisons in the east and Valais in the west. Keeping to the wheel and hub simile, Alpine rivers form the spokes. These have their source at or near the passes. To the east flows the Alpine section of the Rhine; its source is in the Toma lake hidden in a lateral valley of the Oberalp Pass. To the west rises the Rhone at the Rhone glacier which can be walked over from the Furka Pass road. South of the Gotthard Pass lie the headwaters of the Ticino, flowing to Lake Maggiore and the river Po. To the north, gushing down the narrow Schöllenen gorge, flows the Reuss, and not quite symmetrically to the north-west of the "hub" the Aare rises at the Grimsel Pass, linking

Peaks of the Wetterhorn massif (Bern)

the east Bernese Oberland with the upper Valais.

Despite the meandering courses of these five rivers, and although the Rhine and the Rhone are the only two of them which flow through to the sea, and despite nature's lack of absolute symmetry, nevertheless all these five rivers springing from the Gotthard region are of European significance, marking the point where the north-south and east-west barriers converge.


## The Alps – Microcosm and Macrocosm

The varied nature of the Alps is topographically complicated, and even more so as regards their geology, climate and vegetation, not to mention the variety of environments. Still, a few basic characteristics can be distinguished, however simplified such a description must necessarily be. Let us start with the geological structure. Here again the Urseren Valley at the Gotthard Pass is a focal point. Confined in the depths of its valley floor, strata of compressed sedimental rock rose vertically because of the pressures of Alpine crumpling, causing the Swiss peaks to be pushed towards the north. To these belong the Pilatus and the Säntis, mentioned previously. This base zone in the Urseren Valley divides the two main crystalline massifs of the Swiss Alps, namely the Gotthard and the Aare.

Climatically the Alps divide into the differing characteristics of Mediterranean, Oceanic and Continental. That is why there is no specific Swiss climate as such. Switzerland is a climatic reflection of Europe, but the characteristics of the different types of climate vary at the different levels.

The vegetation as a whole, which includes some rare plants, directly reflects the interaction of topography, geology and climate. This does not occur, of course, in any regular pattern, and there exist anomalies which reflect still other specific influences. The *föhn*, this warm current of air flowing down the northern slopes of the Alps over the Alpine chain, accounts for the appearance of Mediterranean species north of the Alps, such as the chestnut and cyclamen mentioned above. We also come across this forest blossom, which does not flower until the late summer, in the mixed deciduous forests dried by the *föhn* in the Rhine Valley of the Grisons, where the climate is very mild, not the Continental climate which we would expect to find because of its location so far to the east of Switzerland. In contrast, the vegetation of the western Valais is not that of an oceanic zone, but at its deeper levels has pronounced continental features, while the influence of the high mountain chains brings about wide variations in temperature and high rainfall. We find the oceanic type of climate, on the other hand, in the damp northern pre-Alps and in the Jura, so far as here, too, the gaps occurring roughly across the general direction of the mountain chain favour a milder climate due to the effects of the *föhn*, light rainfall and the southern aspect of the slopes. Such gaps are those at the edge of the Upper Rhine plain near Basel or on the south-east border of the Jura, where the famous vineyards of Lakes Neuchâtel and Biel are to be found.

Here we have mentioned a few features of the natural basis of the Alpine landscape. It would be quite impossible to describe in a few sentences the cultural basis, and we must therefore abandon any attempt at such a survey, and again refer back to the Gotthard. On the prin-

Ice tunnel in the Rhone glacier (Valais)

A winter's tale in the canton of Vaud                    pp. 60-61

ciple of *pars pro toto,* the journey to the Gotthard may serve to give a historical view of the Alpine experience as representative of the many different cultural aspects of the Alpine landscape.


## Journey to the Gotthard

Anyone approaching the Gotthard from Schwyz or Luzern will notice how the mountains come closer together. The Lake of Luzern takes on the aspect of a fjord inlet and in the Reuss Valley the mountain slopes rise ever more steeply from the narrowing floor of the valley. Only at Wassen do the rocky precipices become less oppressive again and leave enough space for a village and some undulating meadows. The route of the Gotthard railway takes advantage of this to make wide spirals through curves and tunnels in order to gain height before reaching Göschenen. This causes us to pass Wassen three times, first from below, then at the same level and on the third occasion looking down upon it.

Soon after Göschenen, the last station before entering the long Gotthard tunnel, the landscape is almost entirely of vertical dimensions. The rocks rise sheer upwards, leaving no room free for any level ground apart from the narrow space for the foaming Reuss and the ribbon of road; above us is a free opening to the sky where, on a clear day, light penetrates as if from another world.

Now we are in the Schöllenen gorge which for centuries formed an obstacle to the passage over the Gotthard. *Der Schmied von Göschenen* (The Smith of Göschenen), a book for boys still worth reading, tells how the difficulties of the journey were overcome. The author imagines a muscular youth who contrived to forge iron

chains into the rough wall of rock and thus created the famous *Stiebende Steg* (water-sprayed path), to which the Gotthard soon owed its European importance as an Alpine pass. The topographical features which dictated it, namely the closely-knit mountain chains of the Gotthard massif, made it from then onwards the scene of regular streams of trans-Alpine traffic which have never stopped growing, and in which the country people of Uri played a leading part.

It was a celebrated Uri doctor, Eduard Renner (1891–1952), who recorded the life of his mountain people and the magical aspect of their world. In his book *Goldener Ring über Uri,* a work which has been of the utmost value to historians and ethnologists alike, he wrote:

"The traveller making this journey will certainly have some fine tales to tell! Perhaps modesty will prevent him from mentioning how he managed to avoid a disastrous fall or a terrifying glimpse into the murky depths. It was, in fact, the custom to wrap the traveller in a thick blanket, tie him to a mattress and bandage his eyes, and many were no doubt ready to accept that this was done simply as a protection against the cold.

"In summer the journey was made on foot, on pack-horses or sedan chairs or, at a later date, in the capacious post-coaches drawn by five or six horses up and down through the mountains. Ah! how those yellow monstrosities travelled to the jingle of harness and the crack of whip at a brisk trot round the curves and over the hump-backed bridges! The horse on the outside always seemed to be hovering on the brink of the chasm, and the journey was no less adventurous during the green of summer than it was

Mask from the Lötschental (Valais), symbolizing the natural forces of the Alps

through the winter countryside under its mantle of white!

"We must bear in mind that the Gotthard Pass was the shortest connection between the Po Valley and Central Switzerland, a link between the major commercial centres of Italy, Switzerland and South Germany. In a straight line running north to south, it led from Uri to its bailiwicks and those of the Swiss Confederates. This pass, in touch with almost every community in Switzerland, brought the whole country in direct touch with the riches of far-away territories, and the least intelligent could not fail to be lured away by the many possibilities open to him to either side of the Alps, should he decide that arduous toil in his homeland produced too meagre a living."

Today a railway winds its way through the narrow Reuss Valley up to the tunnel entrance at Göschenen, alongside or crossing the ancient mule track over the Bätzberg which, in the Middle Ages, avoided the Schöllenen gorge. Next to this runs the more modern road, widened on several occasions which, in its turn, now seems old-fashioned compared with the ambitious achievement of the present age, the national motorway with its sweeping curves and many tunnels. It now only requires a light pressure on the accelerator in a comfortable car to travel without noticeable effort up the gradients of the northern approach to the mouth of the Gotthard road tunnel. When completed, it will enable the motorist to speed as quickly under the mountain as the passenger has been doing through the parallel rail tunnel. Something of the romantic impression of the landscape is lost, however, by this effortless, rapid travelling. Will it remain lost for ever? It seems as if it cannot be eradicated in so far as we are willing to re-experience it through personal effort and bodily exercise. A walking

Stop-signal from the 1870 regulations of the Swiss Federal Railways

be standing in the way of the route planned for the motorway, there were two alternatives; it would either have to be blown up or moved at considerable expense. The majority of the population voted in favour of preserving and removing the stone, although there were some who voted against this proposal on the grounds that the mountain canton of Uri had more urgent use for its limited financial resources than to save one particular boulder among the thousands of others like it nearby. Was it entirely a sense of reverence and sentiment that caused this financially weak canton to decide in favour of saving the stone where common sense would have dictated otherwise? Perhaps it was rather the instinctive reaction that recognizes that when a piece of one's homeland is destroyed, something is lost from the meaning of life.

Alpine Magic

Just as the people of the Alps have influenced their landscape by clearing forests, fertilizing meadows and removing from the pastures the stones and brushwood brought down by avalanches so, in the reverse sense, the landscape has also influenced the people and their way of thinking. Eduard Renner has described the uncanny behaviour and outlook of the mountain folk in relation to their environment, expressed in a rich collection of legends and tales. One of them tells of a shepherd who, out of boredom, throws stones at a weasel and in a twinkling is besieged by thousands of these tiny animals, an uncountable mass of them which could never have existed there. No one can tell where they came from or where they disappeared to.

"On an unusually clear day somewhere along the military road the whole herd of cattle grazing on an Alpine meadow disappears before the

tour along the old mule track below enables one to recapture the atmosphere of those distant times – scrambling up the *Stiebende Steg,* the legends of the Devil's Bridge and the Devil's Stone and the romance of horse-drawn coaches clattering up and down the twisting gradients.

In the first section we affirmed that the landscape is related to a subjective experience, a relationship which is destroyed when we race through it in a car. Nevertheless there must be something of the *genius loci,* that powerful influence which has always been exercised down the ages by a particular place; otherwise it is difficult to see why the Uri people should recently have decided to save the Devil's Stone, a lump of rock weighing 1018 tons, around which an ancient fable is told. When it was found to

eyes of the herdsman. This hardly causes him any feeling of surprise and he continues as usual, so the story goes, cracking his whip, shouting orders and calling out; and behold – at the next bend of the road there the animals are back again!"

Here, instances of supernatural forces are not the subject of folklore or of any peculiar religious practices. They permeate everyday life when, for instance, the herdsman "fails to behave as usual" or when the prospector has no more time at the end of the day to leave some object in the stone quarry to indicate where he has been digging and, as a result, he finds the next day no trace of either quarry or stones. This is also the case when one talks about the weather with the local inhabitants. They always refer to "It", although one is never sure whether "It" refers merely to the visible weather portents or to some vivid experience of long ago, lost in the mysteries of an omnipotent nature.

I shall never forget one night on the Waldialp, at the back of the Felli Valley when, in the course of a long and exhausting climbing tour on the Schattig Wichel in the Alpine twilight, we were obliged to take shelter from a hailstorm which followed in the wake of thunder and lightning. Shortly afterwards the weather cleared. The skies were still bright, but the meadows were almost entirely in darkness. A herdsman who was with us took a long look all round the bowl of the valley, upwards towards the slopes litter-ed with stones and downwards to the foot of the vertical rock faces. With his experienced eye, with which he could distinguish from far away all the animals in sight, he satisfied him-self that the whole herd was still intact. He then called out the Alpine blessing, consisting of an

The experience of nature in the 18th century at the Herrenbächli water-fall (Lauterbrunnen, Bern). Colour print by Caspar Wolf, 1776 unmelodious tune, amplified by means of a trumpet, and with it describing a wide circle round the whole valley. Feeling like heretics, in some way out of place at watching this ritual, we asked the herdsman why he never once failed to deliver this Alpine blessing. He half closed his eyes, and without relaxing any of his grave expression, told us: "If you don't do it, look out for trouble."

It was only later that it occurred to me that this answer also conveyed something of that indefinable "It" which lies beyond the world we can see and which is not accessible to prayer. "It" is a continuous threat to man, cattle and property. "It" can be the mountain towering above the fertile Alpine meadow, the falls of stone, the foaming mountain torrent, the *föhn* storms and the avalanches. "It" can also be some period of ancient time whose evil powers of sorcery have come to life again, or an accursed patch of ground by the wayside. Woe to the mountain inhabitant who flouts the rituals which protect him from the threats of nature.

Psychologists like C.G. Jung, probing the depths of the human mind, have rediscovered that the "It" is not only related to the external surroundings, but also to the "interior landscape", the human soul. In the legends, figures of speech and customs of our civilization we are gradually brought back into contact with the ancient foundations on which it rests. But in the fine arts, music, writing and painting, the Alpine landscape is also expressed in many varied ways, though these are only recent phenomena. For those country people living in close proximity to their animals, only seldom leaving their valleys, "nature in the raw" has nothing attractive about it. It is a factor in their life which is either neutral or hostile. In the field of literature Jean Jacques Rousseau was perhaps the first to proclaim a reaction against the Age of Enlightenment with his call "Back to Nature!" And since the movement broke away from all that was humanistic, the goal could only be a return to nature at its most primitive; this was to be found in the Alps which previously had been neglected.

The experience of nature which Goethe made in Switzerland in 1775 was much the same as that of Rousseau. However, on his later Swiss journeys, as Richard Weiss has pointed out, Goethe "sought to overcome the gulf which Rousseau seemed to ignore by the affirmation that nature was neither a lifeless, inscrutable object, nor a mere product of the imagination, but identical with man's body and soul. Later still he came to the conclusion that the tragedy of modern man's remoteness from nature had to be resolved by a well-founded union with nature."

Rather different from Goethe, in Schiller's plays the theme of the drama is foremost, the landscape setting on the stage being secondary. In his *William Tell*, the confederates assembled on the Rütli silently meditate in the early morning sunrise on their advantages compared with all those other people "living far below, breathing the fetid air of the towns". In reality, such conceptions are quite remote from the thoughts of the mountain inhabitants, although the above quotation has taken on a new, unpremeditated significance in view of the threats to our modern environment.

Ski run laid out by a caterpillar tractor
At the top of the St Gotthard Pass                    p. 68

## The Alps as a Source of Inner Regeneration

This Alpine experience, formerly the preserve of a few romantic pioneers, developed into a popular enjoyment of nature; the mountain regions, where the sole riches consist of pure air and unspoilt country, became the scene of a flourishing tourist industry. Tourism constituted a major source of revenue from abroad for the whole of Switzerland and a vital element in the economy of the mountain cantons. This was the reason why it was possible for a large number of the local population to go on living in these mountain areas after the coming of the industrial age, surviving the disappearance of the self-sufficient economy of the rural communities, and which made it·no longer necessary for their menfolk to serve as soldiers in foreign armies or to emigrate abroad, as used to be the case.

Today it is no longer a question of the mountains threatening mankind; mankind is threatening the mountains. But many of the summits, mainly the highest among them, and countless uninhabited valleys in the mountains have fortunately been left just as they always have been, or even more lonesome than before; as a rule, the sophisticated tourist, surfeited by the impressions of a hectic age, is unwilling to make the serious bodily effort which is necessary to wander through the more remote regions. But anyone who wants to can seek out these retreats, far removed from the modern communications media, and stay for any length of time he may choose. He will then find himself alone with only his five senses to depend upon and free to commune with the stars, the weather and the perennial changes of day and night.

Men seeking to escape from our over-replete civilization and the security of the well-ordered life of the cities, came to the Swiss Alps and made them the "playground of Europe", as Leslie Stephen called them. The "golden age" of mountaineering, which reached its apogee with Edward Whymper's first ascent of the Matterhorn, gave way to the "silver age"; the series of first ascents up the major peaks was followed by the first climbing expeditions up the large mountain faces and the crossing of the classic ridges. Again it was the enthusiasts from outside Switzerland, most of them Englishmen, who were the pioneers; with the aid of those local guides who later became famous, Joseph Knubel and Franz Lochmatter, Alexander Burgener and Christian Klucker, they opened up the classic climbing routes. To the Englishman Geoffrey Winthrop Young, undoubtedly the leading mountaineer of the "silver age" at the beginning of the 20th century, the mountains meant "genuine adventure". In his book *On High Hills: Memories of the Alps* (1927), he describes the exhilarating climb to a skyline of ridge, where "the connection with lower earth seemed to have been effectively broken. Isolation and the more continuous views, height and our own more protracted effort, all combined to surround us with the remoteness proper to genuine adventure." For Young and countless others, the Alps were the symbol of a mystery, a natural order more enduring than man's. And he aptly added: "Mountains and seas are the largest and best equipped natural training-schools for manhood . . . Even in holiday mountaineering a parting of the ways comes early. We may continue then, if we choose, to treat mountains superficially, as a diversion only for the restless years during which they can succeed in provok-

The golden age of Alpinism: excursionists in the 1860s

A mountain guide of the heroic period: Aloïs Pollinger, about 1880

And if in our present age mountaineering has been inspired more by a desire to break records and a lust for sensation, such as in many of the expeditions to climb the north face of the Eiger with many variations and at all seasons, one should not generalize by dismissing all these efforts as a feverish ambition or simply as a sporting activity. Not a few mountain guides have achieved on their own more difficult ascents, which have never been recorded, let alone accompanied by any publicity. And there are not a few ambitious climbers who have been rescued from the north face of the Eiger by these guides who havc no desire to make the ascent themselves. For them it is no rewarding Alpine achievement. The Italian, Walter Bonatti, who made a lone ascent up the north face of the Matterhorn in the winter of 1965, has affirmed that he was not encouraging anyone else to imitate his way of life. He merely recognized that the mountains offered one possibility out of several to escape from the monotony of our modern age. And because mere repetition was unable to present any opportunity for further development, it was necessary continually to seek new experiences and risks of a different kind. For many it is a case of feeling the necessity of doing something without which there is ultimately no real freedom, no real satisfaction in life and no personal sense of fulfilment. This possibility still exists in the unexplored mountains, where the difficulty of the ascent depends on one's own experience and personal capabilities. For one, the "Alpine experience" begins with a walk along a lonely footpath, for another it begins only when he can pit his own faculties against an unexplored location on some face of rock or ice. For both, though, the motto which is carved in weather beaten letters on a simple cross at the Oberalp Pass: *Ex montibus salus* (all good comes from the mountains) is still relevant today.

ing our curiosity or our vanity. In that case, we must find our training-ground for manhood elsewhere. Or we may take the whole course in self-discovery and self-discipline. In which case we must expect that mountains will make the exercises progressively more difficult in proportion as the knowledge to which they lead grows increasingly worth having; and we must make every effort on our own part to increase their opportunity of impressing us in diverse ways, and to profit by the impressions. "(Excerpt from "On High Hills", G.W. Young.).

# The Threat to the Landscape

Preservation of the Landscape: A Crucial Environmental Issue for Switzerland

The description of the landscape given on the preceding pages makes it easy to forget that Switzerland is one of the most densely populated countries in the world (1980 census: 6,365,960 inhabitants, or 154 inhabitants per square kilometre). The Central Lowlands are more densely populated than Holland, and the number of people per square kilometre in the canton of Zurich is greater than in Japan.

After the Second World War the population of Switzerland increased every year by a number equivalent to that of an average-sized city. Although the population has now become practically static, 20 or 30 square metres are estimated to be disappearing every minute beneath concrete and asphalt. The area of built up land is spreading, partly because of rising aspirations for better housing and infrastructure, but partly also because of the disorganised way in which new building projects have been located. This has led to waste which carefully planned, purposeful use of the land could very well prevent. This is why in Switzerland the planned utilization of land and the protection of nature are the crucial environmental issues of the day, since the steady process of turning land over to housing, factories, highways, etc. is irreversible. This of course is a worldwide trend, but in Switzerland the lack of available land is particularly acute. Here, land not yet built over is a "raw material" of vital importance, despite the fact that the actual growth of industry and population is restricted to a few areas in the Central Lowlands where extensive conurbations have arisen. In 1880 only one-sixth of the population of Switzerland lived in towns; today four fifths live in localities with over 5,000 inhabitants. At the turn of the century 40% of the population were still engaged in agriculture; today around 7% still earn their livelihood in this way. The concentration of population and industrial activity in the towns on the one hand and the depopulation of rural and mountain regions on the other do not bring, as one might expect, a new equilibrium, for the urban areas spread out further as more of the country becomes uninhabited.

Planning and Control

Lack of control will always entail a waste of energy and materials. In the case of our land, it is being recklessly wasted because, among other

Examples of town-planning in the past: the old town of Bern (left) and Luzern (right)                                   pp. 74-75

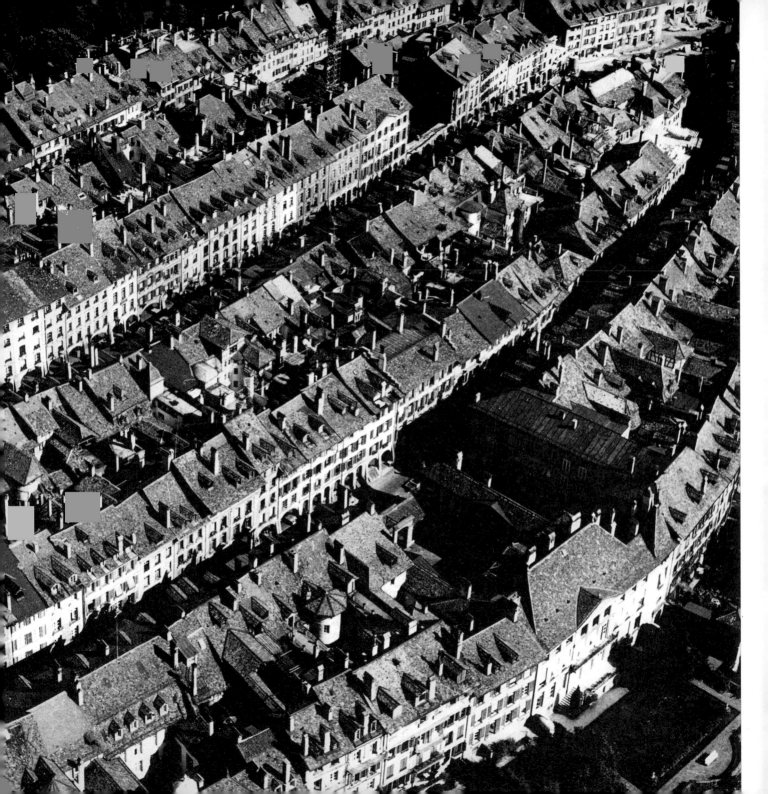

reasons, it does not enter into the profit and loss accounts of the business world; thus it is commonly treated as a disposable commodity, despite the fact that, in Switzerland, it has become for some time an asset in short supply. The Confederation and the cantons have therefore taken steps to check environmental blight and to achieve a balanced rate of growth between different regions.

Planned use of the available land does not mean building more and bigger high-rise blocks. It means, rather, a rational choice of building sites set distinctly apart from the areas which are not to be built over. If the tentacular spread of new housing developments is to be checked, economic controls on a scale hitherto unknown in Switzerland will inevitably be required. Our country is small and landlocked; we have the resources neither of the Dutch, who can reclaim arable land from the sea, nor of the Americans, who have extensive land reserves remaining to be settled and cultivated. Here in Switzerland we are probably closer to the "limits of growth" than we ourselves realise.

The landscape cannot however be measured merely in terms of the area it covers. Its very beauty and worth lie in the immense variety of what grows naturally, or is deliberately cultivated, in it. These are qualities which it would be difficult, if not impossible, to quantify.

As the scenic attractions of the landscape are the most obviously endangered, the Federal Parliament on 17 March 1972 endorsed the federal emergency regulations providing for government controls in the matter of land utilization. This decision marks a new departure in the history of Swiss federal legislation, for it requires the cantons to take action in a non-economic domain in which the cantons had hitherto been free to act on their own initiative; and so this meant some curtailment of that local autonomy which has always been fiercely defended. By the terms of this ruling, the cantons were now compelled, within a period of twelve months, to draw up provisional zoning plans, designating conservation areas where no further building will be permitted in order to preserve not only the natural landscape, but the nation's architectural heritage as well. These urgently needed measures have succeeded in saving many unspoiled stretches of lakeshore, not to mention the landscape in a number of health resorts. They have also enabled the irreplaceable architectural fabric of a number of old villages to be preserved. In other cases where natural landscapes have been in acute jeopardy, where the conflict between the interests of preservation on the one hand and short-term financial gain on the other has been particularly intense, the authorities have steered clear, fearful of turning the question of land utilisation into a dangerously charged political issue. Despite these compromises, the first federal bill concerning land utilisation was rejected when it was put to the Swiss people on the 12th of June 1976, the bill's opponents carrying the day by a meagre 1.9% majority. It was not until the 1st of January 1980 that a new simplified land utilisation bill became law, giving more power to the cantons in deciding on such matters. It is therefore only in the years to come that we shall see whether our federalistic democracy is capable of reading the signs of the times aright and whether or not it will succeed in permanently safeguarding the irreplaceable values of a landscape which, while as yet only threatened in some places, has in others already suffered serious damage.

Industrial blight spreading over the landscape                    pp. 79-80

The Rhine Falls at Neuhausen, near Schaffhausen, and Laufen Castle.
Watercolour, early 19th century

Drastic laws are more necessary today than ever before, but they alone are not enough to achieve intangible aims. The same is true of environmental planning in all its practical applications. Its true success or failure depends not on the rhetoric of its stated aims, but rather on politicians' willingness to put it into practice in everyday political life. If the needed controls are to be effective, it must be recognized that we cannot have both an ever expanding material prosperity and a landscape which is not just a functional environment but also a place of natural beauty and refreshment. In this matter, Switzerland and the other countries of Europe have a momentous decision to make: either they preserve their landscape and with it their inward and outward individuality, or they lose that landscape and that individuality and become meaningless. What is needed today is a sense of civic responsibility, one of whose main effects would be to enable more effective enforcement of the fundamentally sound legislation long since enacted for the purpose of maintaining our landscape and our environment and planning their future. The best examples of such legislation at a Federal level are the Forestry Commission Act (1902), the Game and Wildfowl Act (1925), the Nature Conservation and National Trust Act (1966) and the Waters Protection Act (1972).

The Swiss on his home territory

Sea of fog over the Lake of Luzern p. 84

# SWITZERLAND – VACATIONLAND

Werner Kämpfen

The Landscape: from Image to Experience

Following the description of a "small country with a big landscape" (more than fifty areas throughout the world refer to themselves as "Switzerland" or "Swiss" in some context or other); after a warning and self-critical appeal to care for this landscape and subject it to no further dangers – it would seem appropriate at this point to provide some information about tourism and Switzerland as a vacationland. In other words, from the image to the experience of the landscape. According to modern opinion surveys this remains one of the primary, decisive motives for spending holidays in Switzerland – indeed, for making holiday trips at all.

This movement was introduced more than 200 years ago by Jean-Jacques Rousseau, who liked to call himself "citizen of Geneva." The philosophical, pedagogic and literary works of this "prophet of the revolution" exerted a major influence on many aspects of Western history. I would suggest, however, that the greatest change he brought about was the revolution he initiated in the relation between man and nature – and this was done with reference to the Swiss landscape. Rousseau led the people of his time, trapped under their fancy wigs and in their stuffy salons, "back to Nature" and into Switzerland, which in those days looked in many places like a public park.

Whether chance or sign of the times: the beginning of this Romantic travel movement (Rousseau allegedly invented the word "romantique" by combining "romanesque" and "pittoresque") was influenced by two other great Swiss, Albrecht von Haller of Berne, with his didactic poem about the Alps (1729), and Salomon Gessner (1730-1788) of Zurich, with his fantastic landscapes and idyllic poems. A prominent Rousseau expert called the "lonely walker" the "agent provocateur of Swiss tourism," pointing out that it was after the appearance of Rousseau's novel "La Nouvelle Héloïse," which went into 70 editions, that Switzerland became a world-famous vacationland, indeed the cradle of modern tourism.

For the British conquerors of our Alpine peaks in particular (who were motivated in part by athletic ambition and a sporting spirit) though for others too, the experience of nature, the mountains and the landscape was – and remains – an important factor in deciding on a holiday trip. But in the course of time, and especially in our own age, packaged and minutely organized travel has increasingly transformed the enjoyment of the landscape into rapid-fire sightseeing, a prefabricated consumption which in turn has helped spread the idea of the "consumer landscape." The impulse to orient a district or a vacationland at any price to the needs of tourist mass consumption –

Werner Kämpfen, General Manager of the Swiss National Tourist Office (SNTO), Zurich, from 1960 until 1979

Regatta on Lake Geneva

Jean-Jacques Rousseau, inspirer of the return to nature. Playing-card of the Revolutionary period

placed immediately following the description of the country. However, according to an increasingly widely held view, tourism should be more than just an encounter with the landscape, with a picture-postcard and tourist-oriented Switzerland; a journey to another country should bring with it the discovery of another culture and life style, another political structure and economic view, above all an encounter with different people. Seen from this angle Switzerland's touristic inventory should really have been placed at the very end of these four volumes, after our visitors have already become acquainted with the fundamentals of our political life, economics, culture and style of living. It is only after the discovery of these factors that a genuine touristic encounter with a country can begin.

## A Source of Foreign Currency

From the purely economic point of view the subject of tourism should really be presented after the section covering the other branches of the economy. As more and more people begin to realize, tourism is not an endeavour limited to the operation of hotels and restaurants; whether it serves business or pleasure, tourism is also closely linked to road, rail and air travel, to education, to the textile, shoe, watch and food industries, to agriculture and capital, indeed to virtually all other sectors of the economy. This is why André Siegfried has called it "the fourth dimension of the economy," and why the Americans say: "Tourism is not one industry but all industries." Two details to underscore this point: A substantial proportion of all overnight

this is the danger threatening national as well as international tourism. Because it is nourished largely by the landscape as its basic substance, tourism must not waste, overpopulate or overfurnish the landscape, lest the midwives of tourism become its grave-diggers, and tourism should end up killing itself off. From this viewpoint — the juxtaposition of the experience of a landscape and the threat to its continued existence — this chapter on "Swiss tourism" is appropriately

Pioneers of Alpine tourism. Pen drawing by Rodolphe Toepffer, early 19th century

stays registered in Canton Vaud are in private schools and institutes of learning (which illustrates tourism's link to the realm of education); and in many of the country's major ski-resorts, on a single New Year's night, telephone conversations with other countries regularly run into hundreds of thousands, perhaps even a million francs (which illustrates the financial worth of tourism to the telephone service).

I regard the greatest value of tourism as the opportunity each year to encounter people of every race, religion and political conviction, to show them Switzerland and Swiss, without lengthy monologues but simply through our being as we are. I intentionally place this statement of tourism's great idealistic mission – the facilitating of international and interpersonal relations – ahead of the concrete mercantile data now to be enumerated. In 1981 foreign tourism yielded earnings of 7.8 billion francs, to which were added 5.5 billion from domestic tourism – a total of some 13.3 billion francs or around 8% of Switzerland's total national income. The earnings from foreign tourism break down to a per capita figure of nearly 1,200 francs for every Swiss – doubtless one of the highest figures in international tourism. But it should be noted that, on a per capita basis, Switzerland also spends the highest sum for travels abroad. Its earnings from foreign tourism of 7.8 billion francs are counterbalanced by the 5.3 billion which the travel-happy Swiss spend abroad each year. The Swiss are one of the world's greatest travelling nations, with an average of 1.6 travel holidays per inhabitant per year according to a survey of a representative cross-section of the population. Thus the Swiss vacationland gives as well as it takes. Nor would it ever consider placing obsta-

Fresh air and exercise: a Genevese boarding school about 1840. Enamel on a snuff-box

90

Dried flowers. Ornamental letter from a Romantic album

try or an entire continent. Even in a vacation-land such as ours, tourism must fight for its economic recognition, must ceaselessly try to make this "invisible export" visible. The surplus of some 2.5 billion francs in the "tourist balance of payments" covers more than a third of Switzerland's chronic trade balance deficit. Earnings from tourism tend to benefit primarily the economically weaker parts of the country, particularly the mountain regions.

## From the History of a Vacationland

In view of the fact that because of international tourism today – sometimes regarded as the number one growth industry – entire resorts are created within just a few years, indeed some agrarian and industrial states are turned into tourist countries, a very condensed presentation of the slow, organic growth of Switzerland as a vacationland may be in order for comparative purposes. Tourism in Switzerland has developed largely as a result of private initiative, so that the state has been able to keep influence and occasional supporting actions to a minimum. The fluctuating fate of Swiss tourism, its fat and lean years, can serve as a salutary reminder of this economic sector's sensitivity to crisis. Our historical sketch cannot embrace medieval tourism (e.g., pilgrimages to holy sites; in the 15th century, for example, Einsiedeln was often visited by more than 200,000 pilgrims a year) but it must include spas and hot springs, of which some 85 all over Switzerland provided a mixture of healing and pleasure as early as in the Middle Ages. In those days

cles in the way of its citizens' wish to travel abroad. All that is done is to suggest to the travelling Swiss an alternation between vacations taken at home and abroad, with the slogan: "After every trip abroad, travel in Switzerland." The leading people in Swiss tourism have always advocated the principles of freedom of movement and mutuality and have called for the elimination of every kind of travel restriction.

Our foreign guests, who at the very first contact are often eager for information on the important role which tourism plays for Switzerland, should perhaps be made aware that the average Swiss does not like to be reminded of what he may earn from tourism. He reacts more quickly when the sales of a Swiss product on a foreign market – watches or chocolate, for example – drop by a few percent than when he reads that there has been a decline in the number of overnight stays registered by guests from a certain coun-

The Pissevache waterfall (Valais) about 1820. Watercolour by Gabriel Lory

Baden alone served more than 1,000 people per day, who came to its 30 springs seeking cures for their ills as well as hedonistic pleasures. After Jean-Jacques Rousseau's era came the age of "Bildungsreisen," educational travels designed to broaden the scope of youthful theologians, politicians and literary figures. But the actual "golden age of tourism" began when people overcame their fear of the Alpine world and first climbed the highest peaks of the Alps, Mont Blanc, the Jungfrau, the Matterhorn – feats performed principally by Englishmen with the skilled support of experienced Swiss mountain guides. Other key developments ushering in the real age of tourism were construction of the first steamships, the development of steam engines and railways, and above all the expansion of the Swiss hotel system initiated by pioneers and founders of hotel-keeping dynasties – not to mention the first organized tours of Switzerland put together by Thomas Cook. Conquest of the Alpine peaks, expansion of the railway network and of the hotel system – these are the key headings under which one can find a rich literature on the early pioneer days of Swiss tourism. The nationalization of various private railway lines in order to create the Swiss Federal Railways cost the government a billion francs, an incredibly huge sum in those days. The expansion of the Swiss rail network in the relatively flat midlands was followed by the push into the mountain districts. The impulse for this move was provided by the invention of the cog-wheel railway by Swiss engineer Nikolaus Riggenbach (1817–1899), the builder of the Rigi Railway, whose "Memoirs of an Old Mechanic" ranks among the most remarkable Swiss autobiographies.

Baths and milk cure in Eastern Switzerland in the Romantic period

The energy and organizational talent of a few outstanding individuals brought Swiss hotel-keeping its world renown. Among them was the Seiler family in the Valais; the families Bon, Gredig, Hew and Bezzola in the Grisons; Bucher-Durrer, Cattani, Pfyffer and Frey in Central

The growth of tourism leads to the development of private railways. Uniform buttons of railway employees, late 19th century

The first of the cog-wheel railways: the Vitznau–Rigi line, 1871     p. 96

Z for Zermatt (Valais), made famous in 1865 by the English mountain-climber Edward Whymper     p. 97

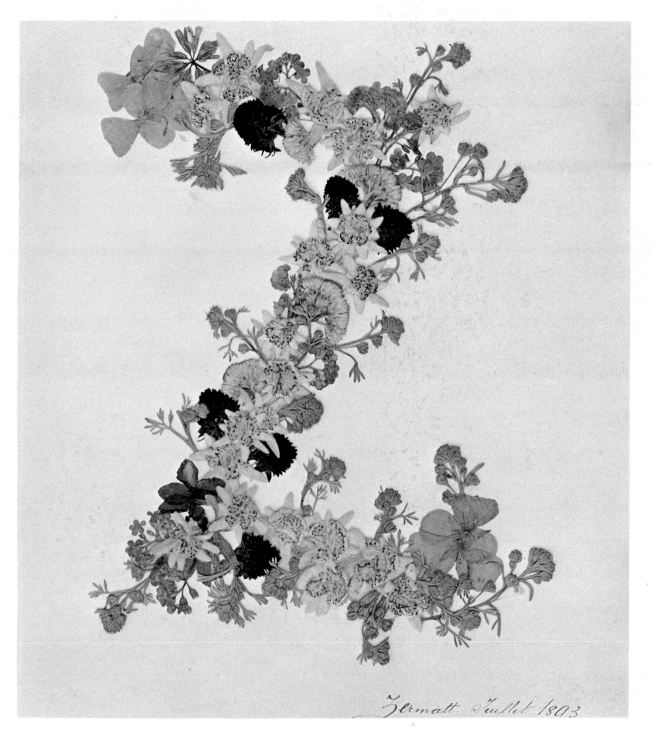

Zermatt. Juillet 1893

Social life in the past: the Hotel Kulm at St Moritz (Grisons) about 1880

Switzerland; Boss, von Allmen and Hofmann in the Bernese Oberland; Chessex and Cherix in the French-speaking part of the country. The way in which prominent hoteliers of that day became "export articles" is illustrated by the unique career of Swiss hotelman Caesar Ritz, whose growing chain of hotels throughout Europe gained him the title "King of the Hoteliers and Hotelier to Kings." The broadly based touristic infrastructure built up in the course of half a century gave Switzerland a leading monopoly position in the world of tourism. According to turn-of-the-century estimates, the average guest spent some 45 days in this country, and foreigners constituted more than 70% of Swiss hotel guests. Today they account for about 50%, and the number of days spent in Switzerland by the average visitor is now only 3.

With the outbreak of World War I tourism came to a half for several years; the internment of (mostly) wounted) soldiers from both sides in Swiss hotels was no substitute and was rather critically regarded as a "humanitarian-commercial" undertaking. This almost devastating setback during the First World War made the Swiss government realize how vulnerable this crucial sector of the economy could be. The up-shot was the founding of the Swiss National Tourist Office (SNTO) as an instrument of economic policy, charged with the task of representing

Panorama of the lower Alps of Central Switzerland from the top of the Rigi (Schwyz). Fish-eye of 1860

The Schlitteda, the traditional Engadine sleigh-ride (Grisons)

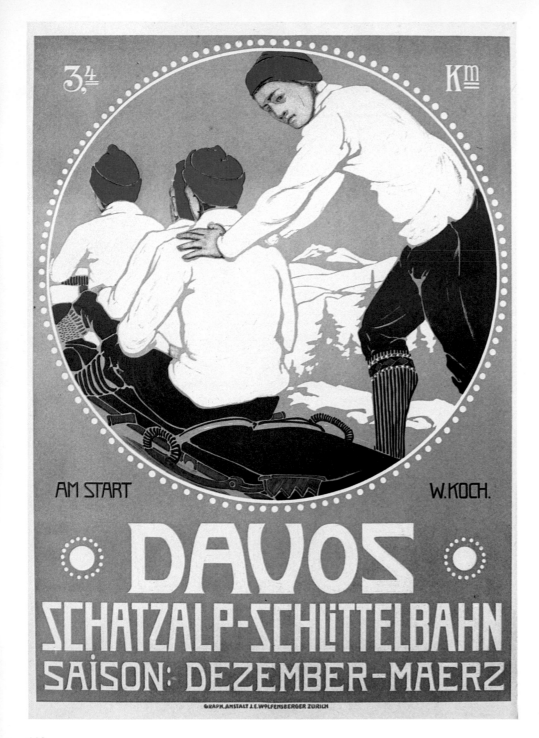

Tourist posters from five decades

SUISSE

REISE DURCH EUROPA · RASTE IN DER SCHWEIZ

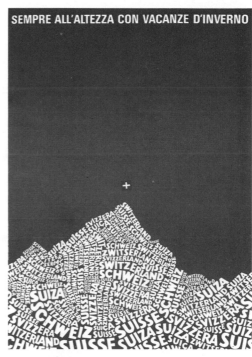

SEMPRE ALL'ALTEZZA CON VACANZE D'INVERNO

Nehmt die Kinder mit!

Kinder reisen jetzt gratis bis zum Alter von 6 Jahren und zur halben Taxe bis zu 16 Jahren. Familienbillete zum alten Preis.

Pour vos vacances... pour vos loisirs

la Suisse

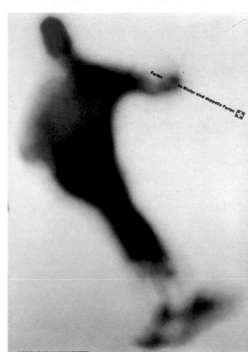

Ferien · Im Winter sind doppelte Ferien

Old inn-sign, 18th century

the Swiss vacationland to the world at large, as well as the Hotel Trust Company Ltd., whose task it was to provide low-cost loans to hotel-keepers in difficulties and thus guarantee the continued existence and modest renewal of these facilities. After a brief upsurge of tourism, the period between the two world wars was overshadowed at the end of the 1920s by the great international economic crisis, leaving Swiss tourism still far behind its former golden years prior to World War I. Neutral Switzerland's total isolation in World War II brought a sudden cut-off of the vital influx of foreign tourists. But at least it was possible to stimulate the Swiss themselves to take their holidays in their own country during this time, so that at the end of hostilities the Swiss hotels could boast the imposing frequency of 15 million overnight stays annually (almost entirely by Swiss guests). Looking back at the period since the end of World War II it is possible to recognize two major phases which strongly influenced tourism in Switzerland:

After 1945, the start of the first phase, an intact Switzerland was eminently suited to gratifying the hunger for foreign travel of visitors from war-torn European states, most especially West Germany. Until into the 1960s we experienced steep growth in tourism and a rising of overnight stays by foreign visitors from 6 to more than 20 million — an advantage which, however, we purchased at the price of a tendency to rest on our past laurels and to only hesitantly set about expanding and renewing our touristic facilities.

Then came the second revolutionary phase in post-war international tourism, which also emanated largely from West Germany: a wave of mass travel — some of it, no doubt, for prestige reasons — bringing about a situation in which a journey to Bangkok became as possible and as inexpensive as a trip to a Swiss resort. This turn of affairs finally prompted those Swiss circles involved in tourism to adopt a policy of more rapid and extensive renewal — in particular an enhanced infrastructure for winter tourism. During this period the growth of overnight stays moved steadily upward, but at a significantly slower pace, partly due to the fact that the limits of hotel capacity had been reached in many cities and major resorts. At the same time great progress was made in modernizing our hotels, making our road and rail networks secure for year-round use and expanding our winter sports facilities (cablecars, ice-rinks, ski runs, etc.).

## The Touristic Inventory

What is the position of the Swiss vacationland today, at the beginning of the 1980's, after the second phase characterized by group tours and mass travel, the end of which seems to be approaching with increasing demands for greater freedom and quality in holidays, a more individual use of free time? Although, in keeping with the standards of our small country, we deliberately avoid outsized facilities, Switzerland's touristic inventory is impressive enough. It includes a dense rail and postal bus network (the latter's routes covering some 8,000 km), continental and intercontinental airports and more than 60 airlines which fly into Switzerland, prominent among them our own "Swissair" (which in 1982 flew to 98 destinations in 66 countries, transporting 7.2 m passengers, 190,000 tonnes of freight and 17,000 tonnes of mail); it also includes a rejuvenated and expanded hotel system, providing year-round service, with the latest in sports facilities and well-marked walking trails. How could one best formulate Switzerland's touristic attractions for our foreign guests?

Using the language typical of travel-brochures, I would say: It is less a land for travel than a vacationland. Compressed into an area of 41,293 sq. kms on both sides of the Alps, Europe's mightiest mountain chain, everything is within reach of a one-day journey: the beautiful peaks of the Alps, rising to more than 4,000 meters in height, and the palms of southern Switzerland, which enjoys a gentle Mediterranean climate at an altitude of only 193 meters above sea level. Within a distance of a mere 200 kms as the crow flies, from Basel to Chiasso the vegetation undergoes a climatic change equivalent to a geographic shift of some 2,000 kms. You can experience polar conditions up on the Jungfraujoch and subtropical conditions in Lugano. The 4,000 meter peaks which tower around Zermatt are on the same latitude as the palms of Como. Davos enjoys more annual sunshine than Nice, which permits our guests to flee the bad weather in just a few hours of rail travel, to escape a biting wind with snow flurries in northern Switzerland by crossing the Gotthard and enjoying the sunshine in Italian-speaking Ticino, or to flee the rain in the Ticino and swiftly move northward to enjoy the brilliantly clear landscape of "Föhn" weather. It is a trip of just a few hours from Central Europe's longest ice flow, the 25 kms long Aletsch glacier, to the mild shores of the Lake Léman. Even in the more open midlands, marked by gentle, forested hills, with their dynamic and busy urban centers, medieval towns and attractive farm villages, and west to the austere valleys of Swiss Jura, the landscape is cut "to the measure of man." With its 50,000 kms of well-marked hiking trails, it would even be possible to see the entire country on foot. The more hasty traveller may entrust himself to one of the punctual Swiss railways in a 5,000 kms network, one of the yellow postal motor coaches with their romantic three-toned horn, or to a readily accessible rented car. The country is covered by an excellent road network, over 60,000 kms' worth, of which there will ultimately be about 1,800 kms of freeway; these highways and by-ways run along lakes and through valleys, over 25 alpine passes, up to the highest village at an altitude of 2,126 meters (Juf, Grisons); on 13 Swiss lakes romantic steamships and more modern passenger vessels ply the waters; 400 cable-cars and 1,700 ski lifts, 8,000 hotels with a total of 280,000 beds, a great number of vacation apartments, chalets, premises for larger groups and camping sites affording accommodation for a further 800,000 people. About 90 ice-rinks, — dozens of outdoor and indoor swimming pools in hundreds of resorts — all these factors help holiday-makers to enjoy meaningful vacations, rest and recuperation as well as physical and mental activity.

So much for Switzerland's touristic inventory, which was greatly expanded and modernized during the 1960s through very big investments.

## Frequencies and Guest Lists

At this point early in the 1980's what is the touristic picture in terms of frequency and the geographic origins of visitors to Switzerland? In the year 1981 our regular hotels, still the key factor in the reputation of a vacationland, registered over 37 million overnight stays, a figure which puts Switzerland up in the top bracket of international tourism. At the turn of the century the Baedeker volumes on Switzerland went through more than 100 editions; today we no longer enjoy a comparable monopoly position. Instead of the former two dozen competitive classical vacation and tourist countries, there are now well over one hundred. The proportion of 60% overnight stays by foreign guests and 40% domestic guests in hotels points to a great dependence on foreign clientele and considerable vulnerability to crises. However, if we also consider the additional 42 million overnight stays registered in 1981 in non-hotel lodgings (vacation apartments, youth hostels, trailer and tent camps, etc.) we have a total of some 79 million overnight stays – a very imposing figure for a small country – and a much more balanced 50-50 proportion of overnight stays by foreign and domestic guests. Naturally this proportion varies sharply from region to region and differs most notably between city and mountain facilities.

A glance at the "more risky half" – i.e., foreign tourism – shows that, in contrast to most other tourist countries, Switzerland enjoys a very balanced geographic mix of markets. Aside from West Germany, which with its apparently inexhaustible reservoir of travellers accounts for about 45%, all the countries coming just behind it (Holland, Belgium, France, UK, USA, Italy) register 3-11%. Thanks to this rather even distribution, and also to a very flexible programme of advertising and public relations, it has been possible in recent years to compensate for the slight ups-and-downs of market figures. Such problems as rapid shifts on the monetary scene, whose devaluations and revaluations can change the price relations between countries and entire continents overnight; the whims of fashion; the increase in the number of families owning second apartments for vacation purposes – all these factors are of concern not only to the Swiss but to the field of international tourism. At any rate the WTO (World Tourism Organisation) in Madrid has now trimmed its prediction for the coming decade in world tourism to an annual growth rate of 5% instead of the previously usual 10%, which means that the number of frontier-crossing tourists will rise during that period from 290 to around 470 million.

## The Trend to Individual Tourism

Following its highly variable fate during the past century, what course does our vacationland intend to steer in the years ahead? The period of expansion and renewal of our touristic facilities is now to be followed by balanced growth, a carefully considered, qualitative growth. Switzerland, which has always tended to give attention to each individual guest, is well served by the increasingly evident trend toward custom-tailored vacations, individually-conceived travel – vacations far from the busy, more populous

Cable-cars in the upper Alps and the thrill of skiing         pp. 110-111

109

centers and travel to more remote places for holidays peaceful or active. All countries engaged in mass tourism are beginning to look more toward the individual guest. We speak primarily of "individual tourism," quite aware that the group business (especially convention and city-tour tourism) provides welcome additional income for our major urban centers and convention resorts. Our country has never put up any barriers to low-cost travel, but has tended to specialize less in large-scale, mass accommodations than in emphasizing family holidays as, so to speak, "individual low-cost tourism." We too have our new vacation villages for the use of foreign organizations specializing in low-cost, mass travel. But back in 1939 here in Switzerland a completely new kind of inexpensive holidaymaking was created with the so-called Travel Fund. It was the device of "travel checks," some given out by employers, and widely accepted at discount prices by railways and hotels, that made a complete success of this kind of "presaved" vacationing; in 1981 the annual turnover of these travel checks was more than 140 million francs.

The phrase "individual tourism" to which Switzerland feels itself committed does not mean simply going off on one's own, not necessarily a "homemade" holiday programme; it can also include a vacation plan worked out by a travel agency or organization. An individual touristic programme may mean: arrival by a money-saving means of transportation, perhaps in a group, but once at the destination everyone is off on his own selected schedule of activity (or inactivity). Our predilection for individual tourism frequently encounters the following objection: How are individualized vacations possible in a country which has an area of only 41,293 sq. kms and is very densely populated? The answer: a good two-thirds of Swiss territory cannot be settled, and large portions of our mountain landscapes, alpine meadows and all our forests have been set aside as natural recreational zones, under government protection since the turn of the century. Moreover the nation's voters have approved new fundamental regulations governing the protection of the landscape and historic structures, regional planning and anti-pollution measures, while a programme of aid to the mountainous districts as well as local and regional planning efforts are aimed at securing for our guests as well as for the Swiss themselves cohesive areas for regeneration and recreation, true landscapes which offer the possibility of enjoying active and health-giving holidays. At the same time it is undeniable that the maintenance of the basic substance of our tourism, our landscape – which, when once lost, cannot be restored – is one of the most urgent and difficult problems of our time. Protection against self-destruction in tourism demands that limits be placed on expansion, demands the insight that the natural beauties and unique qualities of our landscape must not be frittered away.

Nearly always "in Season"

Another reason why Switzerland is especially suited for individual holidays is because it has managed to keep its facilities open and operating all year round. Formerly tourism functioned in high gear only for two or three summer months per year; now it can be truthfully said that Switzerland is nearly always "in season."

Traffic sign: No motor vehicles – Pedestrians only!

Lakeside fireworks in Geneva and night club       pp. 114-115

According to reliable Yugoslavian statistics, on a year-round basis our country has a better rate of hotel bed occupancy than even the southern Mediterranean and other European countries. This is a result of our expanded winter season, which begins in December and often ends only after Easter. In fact, skiing may be enjoyed all year round on our easily accessible, high-altitude ski fields. An increasing number of attractions, largely centering around hiking and walking, is being offered for spring and autumn as well. The greatest difficulty facing this programme of individualized vacations lies in the realm of personnel. Of the 160,000 to 170,000 people engaged in the hotel and restaurant trades, some 70,000 are non-Swiss during the peak season. According to the stabilization policy being pursued by the Swiss government, the number of foreign workers in this country may not be increased. Yet truly individual service to our guests requires adequate staff – a country committed to individualized tourism cannot permit itself to offer service based on throwaway plastic dishes and cutlery. The problem is acute in Switzerland, but it will crop up in all tourist countries in time to come. On the one hand the expansion of the service sector is unavoidable, because greater leisure time creates the demand for more services; on the other hand, the number of people willing to perform such services grows steadily smaller, so that the personnel shortage will soon be felt worldwide in the field of tourism.

In presenting our country as a vacationland the Swiss organizations involved, notably the Swiss National Tourist Office (SNTO) try to treat their task as objectively as possible, although with love for the subject and, where necessary, with ample self-criticism (which is easy to come by among the Swiss); their aim is to inform rather than to propagandize. We would like to present Swit-

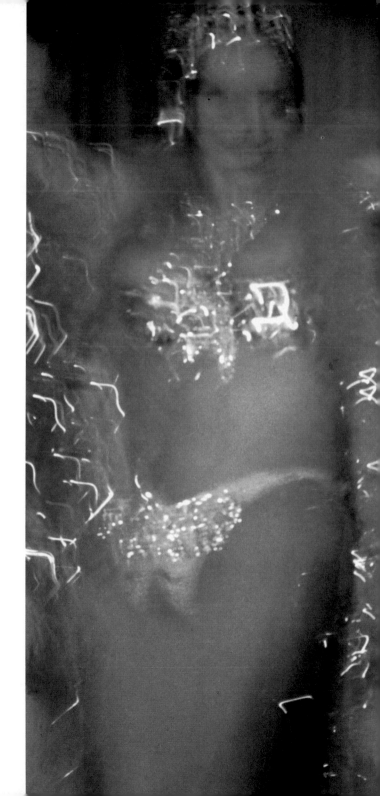

zerland as a vacationland that is *different*, although always conscious of the fact that there are beautiful landscapes to be admired everywhere in the world. For this reason, instead of using hard selling methods, Switzerland issues messages understandable everywhere, inviting people to experience reasonable, rejuvenating and healthy holidays. For a period of ten years, these recommendations and our entire programme were subsumed under the general motto "Roam the Continent — Rest in Switzerland," because we believed that our country is suitable for a longer stay in which there is no need to repack one's valise every 48 hours. In 1962, the "Year of Rousseau", we adopted the slogan "Back to Nature — Back to the Art of Travel". In 1965, the "Year of the Alps", we issued an invitation to "active holidays", after which we sent word to the younger generation that "Switzerland —for the young of all ages". More recently we have drawn attention to the immense variety of special interest holidays Switzerland has to offer—from educational courses of all kinds to summer ski-ing to the decorative painting of rustic furniture. For Swiss tourism the 1980's began with a worldwide campaign based on the simple invitation "Come to Switzerland. It's worth it." At the same time a scheme to promote walking tours in Switzerland was also launched, offering a breadth of possibilities rarely seen in the travel market. The guiding principle for those whose task it is to present Switzerland in this way remains "Performance comes before Promotion". Nothing should be offered unless it is genuinely available, of reasonable quality and priced as stated. By the careful maintenance of quality and the pursuit of balanced price policies Swiss tourism should be able to progress into the future and to do so with confidence. This view is supported by the existence of three trends, all of which are favourable to Swiss tourism. These are:

the continuing development of winter sports, which ensures a better and more evenly spread utilisation of hotel accommodation capacity; the development of holiday apartments, youth hostels, tourist camps, camping and caravan sites as a complement to existing hotel accommodation, and; the growing trend towards more numerous holidays of shorter duration taken in resorts which are closer at hand — Switzerland, located as it is in Central Europe, is in a particularly strong position to benefit from this. By following this future course we shall be making every effort to fulfil modern peoples' need for self-planned, quality holidays.

We are most pleased when our guests get to know not only the touristic points of interest, the Alpine panoramas, the wide vistas from the highpoints of the midlands or the Jura, the charms of our old cities, but also make acquaintance with the other hidden Switzerland, the *Switzerland of the Swiss,* the Switzerland of everyday life. In addition to our 2–300 or so resorts and places of touristic interest there is the wealth of our 3,029 communes, some large and some very small indeed, with their political, cultural and economic individuality. Our country offers countless opportunities to encounter "Mr. and Mrs. Switzerland," who at first glance seem rather remote. Virtually every village or hamlet, even if it numbers no more than a few hundred inhabitants, may be a worthy goal for an excursion, has a proper inn or hotel and one or more historic points of interest, perhaps even a local museum, a handsome church, just as the medium-sized and larger cities have their theaters, concerts and museums. In these small communes it is easy to mix with the people in the evenings, to watch them playing Jass, the Swiss national card game, to hear how the men and women of this country deal with and handle their problems in a democratic fashion, to ex-

Winter landscape in Appenzell. Naïve painting by Albert Manser

perience the unique structure of their national character, their virtues and shortcomings, see how they celebrate their festivals, live with and in their environment, get along with their compatriots of other linguistic traditions. The ex-

perience of this everyday Switzerland can give the visitor as much as, if not more than, an encounter with the purely touristic aspects of the country. And if, after such an encounter, our guests should reach the conclusion that Swit-

Graffito in the Engadine (Grisons)

zerland and the Swiss are different from other countries and other peoples, are uniquely their own, then the purpose of a vacation trip to Switzerland will have been fulfilled – for this is what one expects from such a journey, some-thing that is different, seldom something more beautiful because everyone believes his own country is the most beautiful of all. And this is how we Swiss feel about Switzerland.

# FOCUS ON SWITZERLAND

Series of four volumes sponsored by the
Coordinating Committee for the Presence of Switzerland Abroad

**Editorial board**

Federal Department of Foreign Affairs, Bern
Maurice Jaccard
Frédéric Hool

Federal Department of the Interior, Bern
Max Altorfer
Gerhard Schuwey

Federal Department of Public Economy, Bern
Emilio Moser
Rolf Gerber

Pro Helvetia, Swiss Council for Culture, Zurich
Paul Kamer

Secretariat of the Swiss Abroad
of the New Helvetic Society, Bern
Marcel Ney
Peter Jaeger

Swiss Broadcasting Corporation–
Swiss Radio International, Bern
Lance Tschannen

Swiss National Tourist Office (SNTO), Zurich
Richard Bächi

Swiss Office for the Development of Trade, Zurich and Lausanne
Piero Bardotto

| | |
|---|---|
| Production | Piero Bardotto, Lausanne |
| Chief editor | François Gross, Fribourg |
| Picture research | Nicolas Bouvier, Cologny |
| Layout | André Rosselet, Auvernier |
| Printing | Vontobel-Druck AG, Feldmeilen and Imprimeries Réunies S.A., Lausanne |

Publisher: Swiss Office for the Development of Trade, Lausanne

**Photographic credits**

S. Abelin: 78–79.
L. Bezzola: 74.
N. Bouvier: 2, 4, 16, 20, 54, 72, 98. Bibliothèque universitaire, Geneva: 17, 19, 24, 25, 26, 88. Musée d'art et d'histoire de la Ville de Genève: 56, 77, 89. Musée du Vieux Genève: 90–91. Swiss National Museum, Zurich: slip case, 41, 50, 93, 94, 99. Schlossmuseum, Burgdorf: 40. Zentralbibliothek, Zurich: end papers, 65, 120. M. Dehanne Coll.: 64, 95. H. Fontanet Coll.: 22, 33, 92, 97. I. Niggli: Coll.: 117. D. Wavre Coll.: 23
Comet-Photo AG: 6–7, 80–81, 82
R. Creux: 10–11, 43, 63
Y. Debraine: 12–13, 86
Ph. Giegel (SNTO): 57, 100–101
M. Imsand: 37, 38, 60, 67, 83, 113
H. Kasser: 105
J.P. Landenberg: cover (Swiss National Museum, Zurich)
Len Sirmann Press-Baumann: 111
M. Mathys: 28–29, 46–47
H. Maeder: 106
J. Mohr: 21, 39, 45, 53, 59, 61, 114–115, 118
O. Pfenniger: 68–69, 84–85
O. Ruppen: 8
E. Saxer: 75
R. Schneider: 30–31, 34–35, 48–49, 110
SNTO: 51, 71, 102–103, 107
D. Vittel: 78, 115
D. Zopfi (SNTO): 104
H. Zumbach: 96

| | |
|---|---|
| Translators: | "The Significance of the Landscape", translated from the German by Hendrik P.B. Betlem, Seltisberg "Switzerland – Vacationland", translated from the German by Myron B. Gubitz, Zurich |
| Cover: | Painted silk from Zurich, 18th century |
| End papers: | 16th century map of Switzerland. Woodcut from Sebastian Münster's "Cosmographia universalis" 1954 |

These series of books are published in English, French, German, Italian and Spanish

© 1975 SODT 28 All rights reserved – Printed in Switzerland
1983 2nd edition revised and enlarged/A14327